Savor the Inns of Kansas

Recipes From Kansas
Bed & Breakfasts

Cookbook & Directory

Tracy & Phyllis Winters

Winters Publishing
P.O. Box 501
Greensburg, Indiana 47240

(812) 663-4948

Printed in the United States of America

Cover photograph by: Mil Penner

The information about the inns and the recipes were supplied by the inns themselves. The rate information was current at the time of submission, but is subject to change. Every effort has been made to assure that the book is accurate. Neither the inns, authors, or publisher assume responsibility for any errors, whether typographical or otherwise.

Library of Congress Card Catalog Number 93-61573
ISBN 0-9625329-9-1

Preface

We trust that you will enjoy your journey through the pages of *Savor the Inns of Kansas*, and hope that it might encourage you to travel to some of the Kansas inns presented.

Thanks to all of the Kansas inns that participated. Special thanks to Robert Logan and Robert Cugno of the Kansas Bed & Breakfast Association for their assistance. A variety of inns from across the state is included, and the innkeepers have each provided a favorite recipe.

We have endeavored to provide you with an error-free cookbook and although these recipes are used at the Bed and Breakfasts, they were not specifically tested for this cookbook.

We have used the following symbols to represent the price range of the Bed & Breakfast Inns:

$ - $50 or less
$$ - $51 to $75
$$$ - $76 to $100
$$$$ - more than $100

Please call ahead to verify rates and room availability. Our goal in completing this cookbook is that you may *Savor the Inns of Kansas*!

CONTENTS

123 Mulberry Street Bed & Breakfast

123 S. Mulberry St. • Eureka, KS 67045
(316) 583-7515
Hosts: Jay and Linda Jordan

This Victorian era house nestled in the heart of the Flint Hills, in quiet, rural Eureka, is the perfect setting for a honeymoon, anniversary weekend or mini-vacation. Located 1 hour east of Wichita on Hwy. 54, this 1912 home features your choice of uniquely decorated rooms in "Victorian Dreams", "Country Charm", or "Rosemeade". A cozy parlor with wide screen TV and a hot tub under the stars complete the picture for a relaxing break from everyday life. The peaceful, scenic landscape of the Flint Hills is always a delight. Guided driving tours of historic spots in the area are available. The natural beauty of the Fall River Reservoir and Wildlife Area can also be enjoyed for outdoor recreation. While away quiet hours by horseback riding, golfing and antique hunting, during your refreshing stay.

Rates: $$ Includes full breakfast. Children over 12 are welcome. No pets or smoking, please. We accept MasterCard and Visa.

Jay's French Toast

4 eggs
1 cup milk
1 tablespoon granulated sugar,
honey or maple syrup
1/4 teaspoon salt
1 teaspoon ground cinnamon
1 teaspoon freshly grated nutmeg
1 tablespoon minced fresh tarragon or
1 teaspoon dried tarragon, crumbled (opt.)
1/2 teaspoon vanilla extract
8 slices (1 1/2" thick) day-old French
bread, sweet or sourdough
1/2 cup (1 stick) unsalted butter
Powdered sugar for dusting
Parsley to garnish

In large bowl, combine eggs, milk, sugar or other sweetener, salt, cinnamon, nutmeg, tarragon, and vanilla. Beat until well mixed. Dip bread slices into mixture, turning to thoroughly coat both sides. Heat 2 tablespoons butter in skillet over medium heat until foamy. Add half of the bread slices and cook until golden brown on each side, turning once and adding additional butter as needed. Cook remaining dipped bread in the same way. Dust with powdered sugar and serve hot with your favorite topping and garnish with parsley.

Makes 4 servings.

Balfours' House Bed & Breakfast

Route 2, Box 143 D • Abilene, KS 67410
(913) 263-4262
Hosts: Gil and Marie Balfour

In a fast-paced world you deserve a comfortable retreat designed to soothe your senses and restore your spirits, in a contemporary country home where you can kick off your shoes, and relax! Main house offers indoor swimming pool and spa. Suite with private entrance has two bedrooms with one queen and one full size bed, and bath. Large comfortable living area allows you to watch color TV/VCR, read in front of the natural stone fireplace, or play the piano. This area also provides additional sleeping space. Separate bungalow decorated in southwestern style is completely private, including a bath and large comfortable area to relax on futon couches. Studio layout is ideal for romantic retreats or family getaways. Queen bed, and couches make into queen and full beds. Enjoy continental breakfast with varied menu served poolside or on outdoor patio.

Rates: $ - $$$$ Includes continental plus breakfast. Children are welcome. Pets allowed. No smoking, please. We accept MasterCard and Visa.

Mamie Eisenhower's Sugar Cookies

1 1/2 cups flour
1 teaspoon baking powder
1/2 teaspoon salt
1/2 cup butter
1 cup sugar
2 egg yolks, well-beaten
1 teaspoon vanilla extract
1 tablespoon cream
Granulated sugar for tops

Mix and sift flour, baking powder and salt. Cream butter, add sugar slowly and cream until fluffy. Stir in well-beaten egg yolks, and vanilla extract. Add sifted dry ingredients alternately with cream. Chill for one hour, roll and cut into any desired shape. Sprinkle with sugar before baking. Bake in moderate oven at 350° or 375° for 10 - 12 minutes.

The Barn B&B Inn

Route 2, Box 87 • Valley Falls, KS 66088
(913) 945-3225
Hosts: Tom and Marcella Ryan

The Barn B&B Inn opened its doors to guests on March 30, 1986. At that time there was some doubt whether anyone would want to spend the night in a renovated barn. 7 years and 20,000 guests have answerd that question in the affirmative. It is a real 100 year-old barn. It was first designed with horse stanchions and a milking parlor and provided a roof for the year's hay crop. It served as a pig farrowing house just before it became an inn. We have been told that the U.S. Cavalry used to water their horses at a nearby spring and that Buffalo Bill Cody slept here with his horse. Come enjoy the peace and quiet of the countryside and some rest and relaxation, in one of our 20 guest rooms, our 2 new living rooms and indoor heated pool. Savor our rural charm and scenic beauty!

Rates: $$$ Includes full breakfast. Children are welcome. No pets or smoking, please. We accept MasterCard, Visa, Am Ex and Discover.

Mexican Crazy Crust

Crust:
1/2 cup flour
1/2 teaspoon salt
1/2 teaspoon baking powder
1/4 cup Crisco
1/2 cup sour cream or yogurt

Filling:
1 lb. ground beef, browned
1/2 cup chopped onion
1 teaspoon salt
2 teaspoons chili powder
1/4 teaspoon hot pepper
16 oz. can pinto beans, undrained
6 oz. can tomato paste

Topping:
1/2 cup shredded lettuce
1/2 cup chopped tomato
1/2 cup shredded Cheddar cheese

Preheat oven to 425°. Combine crust ingredients. Spread batter in greased and floured 9" - 10" pie pan. Spread batter thinly on bottom, thicker on the sides. Brown ground beef with onion and drain. Add remaining filling ingredients. Pour over crust. Bake for 20 - 30 minutes or until crust is a deep brown. Remove from oven and top with tomato, lettuce and cheese.

Makes 4 servings.

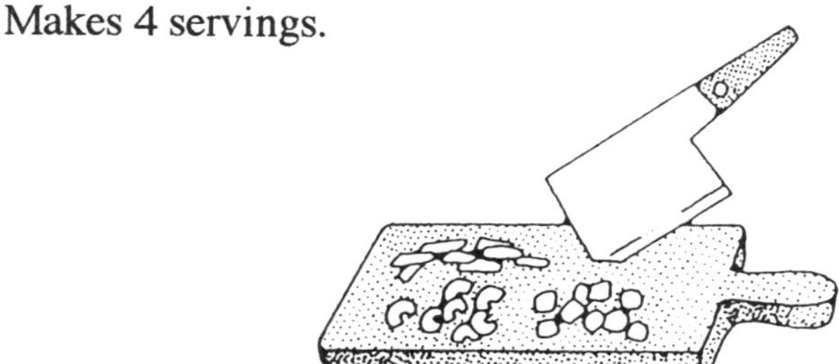

Bedknobs & Biscuits

15202 Parallel • Basehor, KS 66007
(913) 724-1540
Hostess: Sonnie Mance

A country Victorian interior, a brown brick house on a hill, peace and quiet. A comfortable, pretty place to come when you need a vacation or just want a special night's sleep, our king and queen beds await you. Sonnie welcomes you with a refreshing beverage and something from the oven. Breakfast is served at the pine farm table in the big kitchen: juice, fresh fruit, a hot egg dish, meat, two breads, assorted jams, homemade applesauce and a potato dish, served family style. Attend one of our nearby attractions, Renaissance Festival, race track or ampitheater.

Rates: $ Includes full breakfast. Children over 8 are welcome. No pets or smoking, please.

This is an old family recipe.

Danish Pudding

6 eggs
1 quart milk
2 tablespoons flour dissolved
in 2 tablespoons cold water
1 teaspoon vanilla
1 1/2 - 2 cups brown sugar

Beat eggs well. Add milk and flour/water mixture. Add vanilla. Lightly spray 8 - 10 custard cups or heart molds with Pam. Sprinkle brown sugar to cover bottom of each dish. Fill with egg/milk mix. Set in baking pan of hot water. Bake at 350° until knife inserted in center is clean. Chill well. To serve, invert on serving plate. Garnish with a strawberry or other fruit.

Makes 8 - 10 servings.

Bennington House

123 Crescent Drive • Fort Scott, KS 66701
(316) 223-1837
Hostess: Betty Rocher

You will be certain to enjoy your stay at Bennington House, a home with country atmosphere and charm, but also the comfort of modern convenience. Your hostess has a Bachelor's degree in home economics and a Master's degree in special education. She has raised 4 children, and is now retired from teaching. Two bedrooms in this comfortable modern home are available for bed and breakfast use. One is a master bedroom, with queen bed and private bath. The other has a standard bed and shared bath. A full breakfast is served at your convenience, and we pay close attention to special dietary needs. A variety of meals are served, that could include seasonal fruits, eggs, bacon, sausage, muffins, cinnamon rolls, and many traditional breakfast meals. Our motto is: "A Bennington Guest Deserves the Best."

Rates: $$ Includes full breakfast. Children over 4 are welcome. No pets or smoking, please.

Homemade Vegetable Soup

1 tablespoon unsaturated oil
2 stalks celery
2 carrots
1/2 red onion
2 - 3 green onions
1/2 small zucchini
1/2 lb. ground beef or turkey
2 cans stewed tomatoes

Chop all vegetables to desired size and stir fry in unsaturated oil. When they are crisp-tender, remove from oil. Sauté beef or turkey, and drain if needed. Add stewed tomatoes to meat. Heat to boiling, then add vegetables. Serve hot, but before vegetables are soggy. Other leftover vegetables or meat can be added as well. You may add a can of vegetable or beef soup for added flavor.

Makes 6 servings.

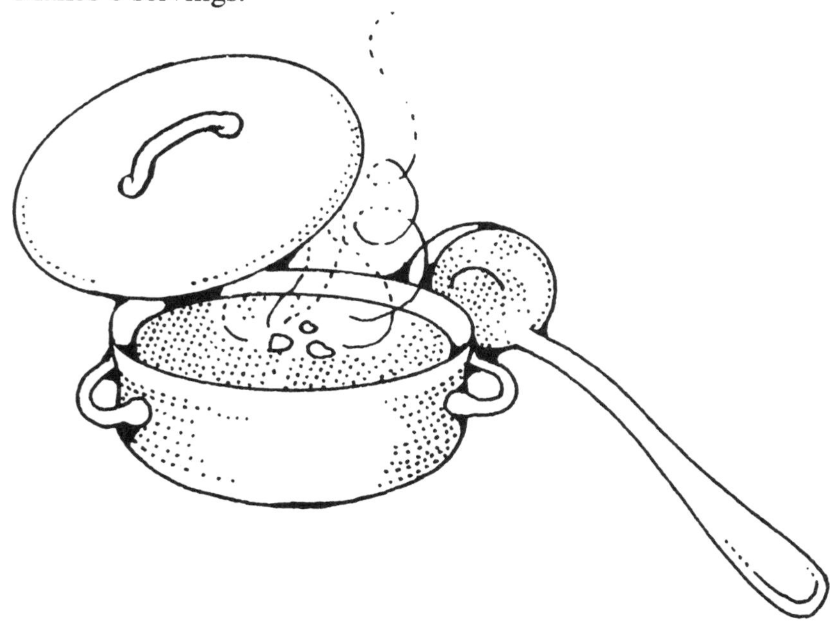

The Chenault Mansion

820 S. National • Fort Scott, KS 66701
(316) 223-6800
Hosts: Bob and Elizabeth Schafer

We invite you to take a step back in time to when graciousness was a daily routine, in an elegant home where little has changed since 1887. Visit in the Victorian parlor, sleep in a period room, and have a full breakfast under one of the crystal chandeliers. Curved glass windows, stained and leaded glass, ornate cherry, gum, ash and oak woodwork, pocket doors, and fireplaces. Furnished with antiques and a large china and glass collection accumulated by your hosts over the years. 5 guest rooms, each named after a notable resident of the mansion, have been decorated in the era & personality of the namesake. Antique and vintage furnishings create a unique and peaceful haven. Private baths with showers, thirsty towels, a/c, and queen sized beds. From the first glimpse, you begin to feel the mansion's charm and personality. The double cherry doors are opened by your hosts, and you know your stay will be a special experience. Hospitality is not just our business, it's our way of life!

Rates: $$ Includes full breakfast. Children are welcome. No pets or smoking, please. We accept MasterCard, Visa, and Discover.

This cake only uses half a can of pie filling. It might be wise to make two coffee cakes and freeze one, or freeze the leftover pie filling for later use, so it doesn't occupy space in your refrigerator for months.

Cherry-Almond Coffee Cake

2 cups all-purpose flour
1 teaspoon baking powder
1 teaspoon baking soda
1/2 teaspoon salt
8 tablespoons (1 stick) butter
1 cup granulated sugar
2 large eggs
1 teaspoon vanilla
1/2 teaspoon almond extract
1 cup sour cream
1 cup cherry pie filling (or any variety of fruit)
1/2 cup (1 3/4 oz.) natural almond slices

Heat oven to 350°. Butter 9" springform pan. In small bowl mix flour, baking powder, baking soda and salt well. In large bowl, beat butter with electric mixer until creamy. Add about 1/4 cup sugar at a time, beating after each addition. When mixture is light and fluffy, add eggs, one at a time, beating after each addition. Beat in extracts. Scrape side of bowl. With mixer on low, add flour mixture, about 1/2 cup at a time, alternating with about 1/3 cup of sour cream at a time, beating just until batter is smooth. Spoon about 2 cups batter into prepared pan, add half the cherry pie filling, and swirl it once through batter with a rubber spatula. Spoon remaining batter evenly over top, then remaining cherry pie filling (but don't swirl it). Sprinkle with almonds, press almonds lightly into surface. Bake 60 - 65 minutes or until cake is brown on top and shrinks slightly from sides of pan, and wooden toothpick inserted in center comes out clean. Cool in pan on wire rack for 15 minutes. Remove pan sides. Serve cake warm.

Makes 12 generous servings.

The Cimarron

Box 741 • Elkhart, KS 67950
(405) 696-4672
Hosts: Kyle and Linda Martin

Located at the crossroads of Kansas, Oklahoma, and Colorado, our home is located only a few miles from the scenic and historic Cimarron National Grasslands, along what was once a portion of the Cimarron Cutoff of the Santa Fe Trail. The rural setting provides a quiet respite for the traveler or hunter. Our home becomes yours as you enjoy more than 3,600 square feet, which includes a full shared bath, three guest rooms, and a spacious recreation room complete with TV, VCR, and a regulation size pool table. In the fall enjoy dove, pheasant, and quail hunting.

Rates: $ Includes full breakfast. Children are welcome. No pets or smoking, please.

Overnight Omelet

1 lb. sausage, browned and drained
5 eggs, beaten
1 1/2 slices bread
2 cups Cheddar cheese
12 oz. can evaporated milk

Brown sausage and drain. Beat eggs and milk, add torn bread pieces, cheese, and sausage. Pour into 9" x 13" x 2" baking dish. Cover with foil and refrigerate overnight. Bake at 350° for 45 minutes.

Makes 8 servings.

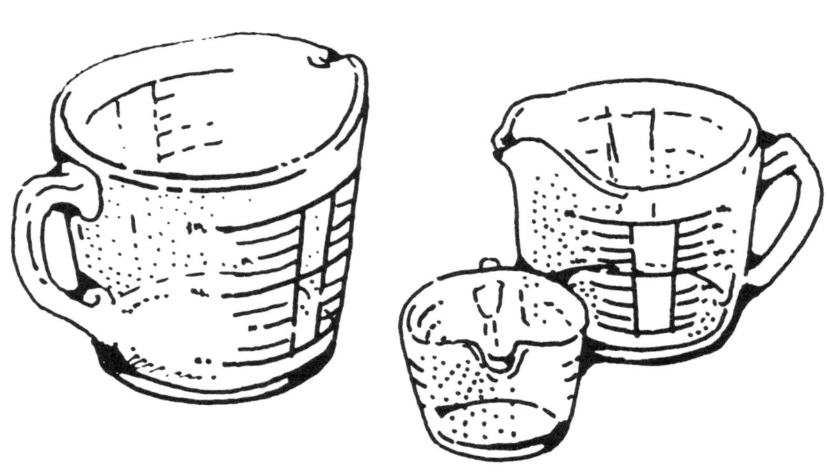

The Cottage House Hotel

25 North Neosho • Council Grove, KS 66846
(316) 767-6828
Hostess: Connie Essington

Lovely example of Prairie Victorian architecture. Twenty-six rooms furnished with some antiques; each room is different. Modern comforts - hotel has been completely renovated, keeping the best of the old. Some rooms have old-fashioned bath tubs, all have showers, some have whirlpool tubs. Two-story building, all rooms have private baths. Downtown in historic Council Grove, on the Old Santa Fe Trail. Cable TV, direct dial phones, gift shop, conference room. Near 2 lakes, and country club golf course. Interesting shops downtown.

Rates: $ - $$$ Includes continental plus breakfast. Children are welcome. Extra $8.00 charge for pets. 8 non-smoking rooms available. We accept MasterCard, Visa, Am Ex and Discover.

This recipe is so EASY! You can use your favorite flavor of sherbet.

Punch

46 oz. can unsweetened
pineapple juice
2 - 33.8 oz. bottles ginger ale
3 quarts raspberry sherbet,
softened (or other flavor of choice)

Mix all ingredients together and serve immediately.

Serves 30.

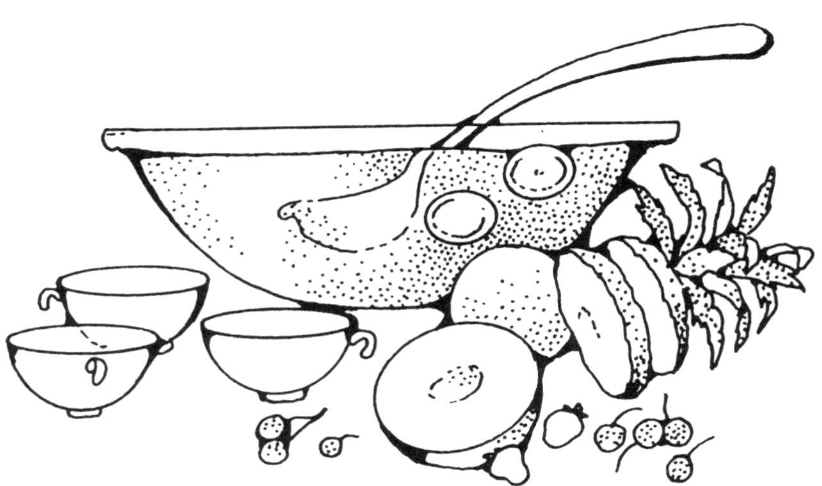

Country Corner

Box 88, South Highway 25 • Atwood, KS 67730
(913) 626-9516
Hosts: Charles and Connie Peckham

Wake up to a country fresh morning without going to the country. Large two-story home located where town and country meet. Whether you choose to enjoy a quiet walk down a country lane or relax next to the large fireplace, you are sure to feel at home. The home is decorated with antiques and many family heirlooms, tastefully blended with hand-crafted items. All guest rooms are on main floor and are handicapped accessible. Discounts for children 18 and under.

Rates: $ Includes continental plus breakfast. Children are welcome. No pets or smoking, please.

Breakfast Pull-Apart

1/2 - 1 cup chopped pecans
24 dinner rolls, frozen
3/4 cup brown sugar
2 teaspoons cinnamon
3 oz. pkg. regular vanilla
pudding (not instant)
Margarine to taste

Grease bundt cake pan and scatter pecans on bottom. Place rolls in single layer, lining up sides as well. Sprinkle brown sugar, cinnamon and dry pudding mix over rolls and place thinly sliced margarine pieces over all. Cover and let rise several hours or overnight. Bake at 350° for 30 minutes. Invert onto plate while hot.

Country Dreams

Route 3, Box 82 • Marion, KS 66861
(316) 382-2250
Hosts: Kent and Alice Richmond

Come share our new country home overlooking a 19 acre lake and 480 acres of scenic beauty and wildlife. Fishing, hunting, boating and hiking activities are available. Five guest bedrooms with private baths, queen size beds, and a/c. A full country breakfast is served. Other meals may be arranged in advance. Guests are welcome to use our meeting rooms, satellite TV, VCR, movie tapes, and refrigerator. Additional group lodging is available in a nearby 4-bedroom house with shared bath, 3 queen and 2 single beds, and cooking privileges. Our facilities are available for business meetings, social events and special dinners, with home cooking catered to your special needs (min. 10, max. 75). Located 7 miles east of Junction 56 and 77 on Highway 150, then 3 miles north. Come, relax, and enjoy the peace and quiet of country living.

Rates: $$ Includes full breakfast. Children are welcome. Pets allowed in kennel. Smoking allowed in lodge only. We accept MasterCard and Visa.

This recipe has been a family favorite for years, and is something different to do with plain old green beans.

Barbecued Green Beans

4 strips bacon
1/2 cup diced onion
3 cans French style green beans,
well-drained
1/2 cup catsup
1/2 cup brown sugar, packed
1 tablespoon Worcestershire sauce

Place bacon in baking dish, cover with waxed paper, and microwave on high for 5 minutes or until crisp. Remove bacon and drain on paper towels. Sauté onion in bacon grease for 3 minutes. Add catsup, brown sugar, and Worcestershire sauce to the sautéed onions and mix. Add drained green beans and stir gently. Top with crumbled bacon. Cover. Bake at 325° for 2 hours.

Makes 8 servings.

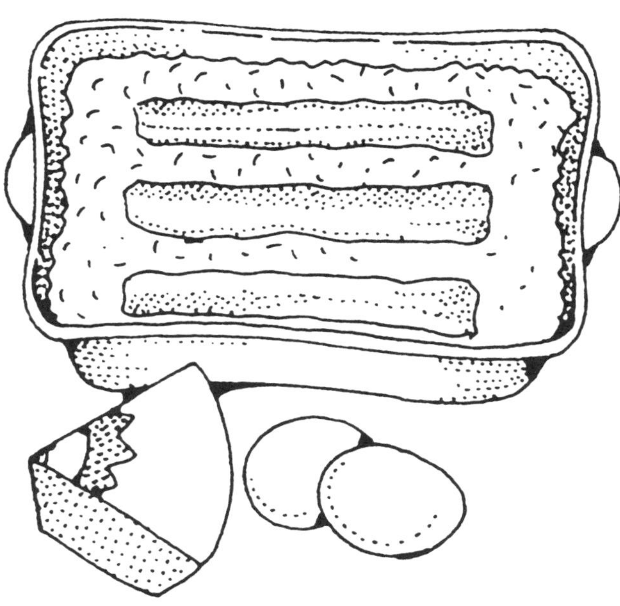

Country Inn

3871 198 m • Dorrance, KS 67634
(913) 666-4468
Hosts: Mary Ann and Richard Steinle

Early 1900 home in original condition, in small-town setting, at Exit 199, on I-70. With no traffic noise, there's nothing to do but sit on the porch, and listen to children playing and birds singing. Fall asleep to the sound of a gentle breeze blowing through big, old cottonwood trees. Good hunting and fishing. Near Lake Wilson.

Rates: $ Includes full or continental plus breakfast. Children allowed by permission only. No pets or smoking, please.

Pineapple-Carrot Muffins

1 cup white flour
3/4 cup whole wheat flour
1/2 cup brown sugar
1 teaspoon baking soda
1 teaspoon cinnamon
1/4 teaspoon salt
1/2 cup oil
8 oz. crushed pineapple, undrained
1 egg
1 cup shredded carrots
1/2 cup raisins
1/2 cup chopped walnuts

Preheat oven to 375°. Grease bottoms of 12 muffin cups. Combine flours, brown sugar, baking soda, cinnamon and salt. Set aside. Combine oil, pineapple and egg in small bowl, blend well. Add to dry ingredients and stir until moist. Add carrots, raisins and nuts. Fill muffin cups 3/4 full. Bake for 18 - 20 minutes. Cool 5 minutes and remove from pans.

Makes 12 muffins.

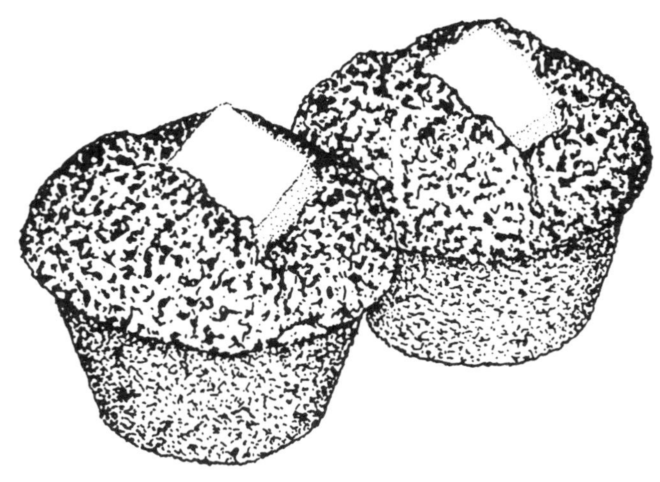

Creek Side Farm

Route 1, Box 19 • Fowler, KS 67844
(316) 646-5586
Hosts: Dean and Mary Reese

Peaceful farmhouse with 2 double bedrooms/shared bath. The 1930 house was built on the banks of Crooked Creek, the site of the post office of the old ghost town of Wilburn. Plenty of pheasant hunting in the fall. Deer also wander around with wild turkeys often seen. Trailer hook-up available and pen for horses. Enjoy greenhouse in spring and perennial garden. Breakfast served on glassed-in porch. Safe for single travelers. 35 minutes from Dodge City and other attractions.

Rates: $ Includes full breakfast. No pets or smoking, please.

A friend gave this recipe to me after she served it at a card party.

Crab Salad

2 cups diced celery
2 cups diced green pepper
1 cup diced onion
3 lbs. crab (imitation or real)
1 cup Hidden Valley Ranch dressing
1 cup sour cream
Chopped lettuce or spinach

Dice vegetables and mix with crab meat. Pour dressing and sour cream over meat and vegetables, and mix lightly. Serve on bed of chopped lettuce or spinach. Also delicious as a spread for crackers.

Makes 10 servings.

The Elderberry B&B

1035 S.W. Fillmore • Topeka, KS 66604
(913) 235-6309
Hosts: Carol and Jerry Grant

The Elderberry B&B is our restored 1887 Queen Anne home in the central Holliday Park area of Topeka. Both of our rooms have private baths and the beds are triple-sheeted. Numerous old hats, hat pins and hat pictures fill the guest rooms as there once was a millinery shop in the home. Original beveled leaded glass windows, massive oak woodwork, pocket doors, family antiques and comfortable furnishings add to the enjoyment and comfort of the guests. Guests are offered a choice of items on a breakfast menu and may eat in the privacy of their rooms or in our dining room, and are served on antique flow blue china and/or depression glass. Elderberries are native to eastern KS and are believed to have magical powers that bring good luck, along with medicinal qualities. We feature homemade elderberry jelly at our breakfasts.

Rates: $ Includes full/continental plus/continental breakfast. Children are welcome. No pets or smoking, please.

This is the favorite evening snack of my B&B guests.

Lemon Squares

1/2 cup margarine
1/4 cup powdered sugar
1 cup flour
2 eggs, beaten
1 cup sugar
2 tablespoons flour
2 tablespoons lemon juice
Grated rind of 1 lemon

Mix margarine, powdered sugar, and flour, and press into greased 8" x 8" pan. Bake at 350° for 20 minutes. Mix together remaining ingredients, and pour over hot crust. Bake at 350° for an additional 20 minutes. It should not brown.

Makes 12 - 15 servings.

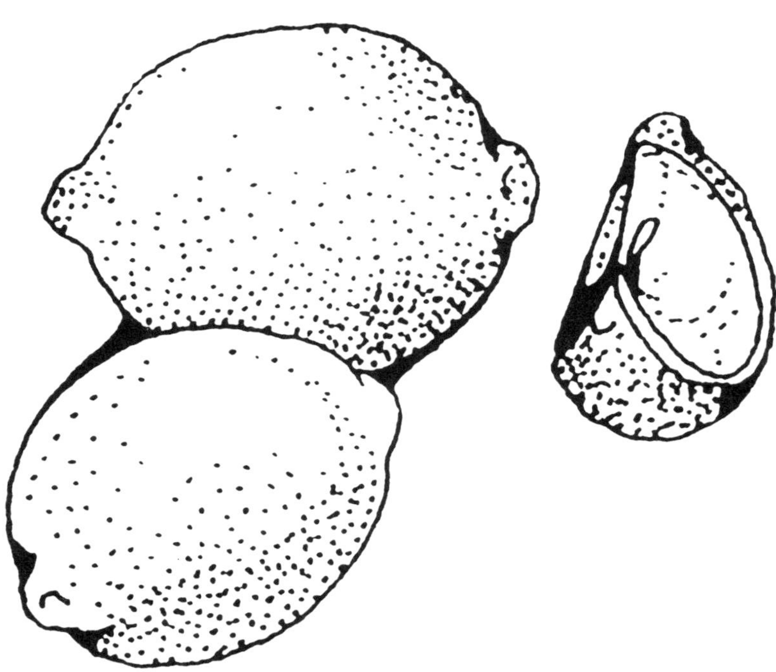

Flint Hills Bed & Breakfast

613 W. Main • Council Grove, KS 66846
(316) 767-6655
Hosts: Merry Barker and Bob Matthews

Flint Hills Bed & Breakfast is located on the Santa Fe Trail in historic Council Grove. The house is an American Four Square built in 1913. It has its original yellow pine and oak woodwork and hardwood floors. Each of the three guest rooms is filled with antiques, has a private bath, and has a personality of its own. You can relax in the TV room, on one of our two large porches, or you may want to stroll our historic downtown. In the morning you are invited downstairs to our dining room to enjoy a full country breakfast.

Rates: $ - $$ Includes full breakfast. Children are welcome. No pets or smoking, please. We accept MasterCard and Visa.

This was sent to me by Mary Simmons after her stay at my B&B.

Oatmeal Pancakes

1 1/2 cups rolled "quick" oats
2 cups buttermilk
2 eggs, beaten
3/4 cup flour
1 teaspoon sugar
2/3 teaspoon salt
2 teaspoons baking soda

Put oats in mixing bowl and add buttermilk. Beat eggs and add to mixture. Mix all dry ingredients together, then slowly add to buttermilk mixture. This will be thick batter, like muffins. Drop by spoonfuls onto hot oiled griddle, about 400°. These pancakes take longer to cook, but are worth the wait! Turn to brown both sides.

Makes approximately 20 pancakes.

The Flower Patch Bed & Breakfast

610 Main Street • Atwood, KS 67730
(913) 626-3780
Hosts: Fred and Karen Gatlin and daughter, Hannah

Enjoy our spacious home in a quiet town; the great room with fireplace to warm you in winter; backyard pool to cool in summer. Stroll through flower and herb gardens, browse upstairs in the "Sweet Annie Shoppe" filled with dried flower/herbal wreaths, fragrant gifts. Learn the technique for primitive style hand hooked wool rugs; supplies and classes available with prior arrangement. Private hunting privileges on our farm property available. Families welcome. Located in northwestern KS farming village/community. Lake for fishing, beautiful golf course, antiques, museum. Two large rooms, each with private bath, queen beds, and an extra room for two if needed. Cable TV. Breakfast served poolside if desired.

Rates: $ Includes continental plus breakfast. Children are welcome. No pets or smoking, please.

This salad is peppery, but great!

White Lake Salad

3/4 lb. romaine lettuce
1/4 lb. fresh spinach
1/4 lb. mushrooms, sliced
2 oz. alfalfa sprouts
8 - 10 slices bacon, fried & crumbled
4 oz. blue cheese, crumbled
2 hard-cooked sliced eggs
6 - 8 cherry tomatoes, halved

Dressing:
Generous 3/4 cup sour cream
1/4 cup mayonnaise
2 tablespoons fresh lemon juice
1 teaspoon Worcestershire sauce
1 beef bouillon cube, dissolved
in 4 teaspoons warm water
4 teaspoons cracked pepper

Combine all dressing ingredients in bowl and whisk to blend. Add milk to thin if needed. Refrigerate, covered, at least 3 hours. May be kept in refrigerator up to 10 days. Mix romaine and spinach in large salad bowl. Add mushrooms, then dressing, and toss well. Top with sprouts, crumbled bacon, blue cheese, egg slices and tomato halves, arranging in concentric circles. Or you may toss all ingredients together with dressing.

Makes 6 - 8 servings.

Fort's Cedar View

1675 West Patterson Ave. • Ulysses, KS 67880
(316) 356-2570
Hostess: Lynda M. Fort

Started in 1987 as a bed and breakfast by it's owner-designer, the home was finished in 1978 after 3 years of landscaping and construction. The 20 acres surrounding the Inn are tree lined and encourage songbirds and wildlife. Located in agriculturally rich Grant County, on top of the largest natural gas reserve in the world. The home was the center of busy family life, with 5 children in many activities including competitive swimming, thus an indoor swimming pool is kept heated for your enjoyment. Breakfasts are served suited to our guests' needs. No evening meals are available at the Inn. Ulysses, the only town in the county, is located 8 miles north of famed Wagon Bed Springs. The Grant County Museum and restored Edwards Hotel give you a glimpse into the development of irrigation, transportation, agriculture, and ranch life.

Rates: $ - $$ Includes continental plus breakfast. Children are welcome. No pets or smoking, please.

An excellent fruit dish to serve for breakfast or served with a wafer for dessert.

Fruit Slush

6 oz. frozen concentrate pink lemonade
6 oz. frozen concentrate orange juice
10 oz. frozen strawberries, quartered
20 oz. crushed pineapple with juice
6 bananas, sliced or mashed
2 - 12 oz. cans 7-Up

Cut strawberries when slightly thawed. Defrost lemonade and orange juice, stir together. Add other ingredients, including strawberries, mix well and dip into plastic punch cups. Cover with Saran Wrap or foil and freeze. To serve, remove from freezer to refrigerator the night before serving, or leave at room temperature for approximately 3 hours.

Makes 16 servings.

Hawk House Bed & Breakfast

307 W. Broadway • Newton, KS 67114
(316) 283-2045
Hosts: Lon and Carol Buller

The Hawk House was built in 1914. The home has oak woodwork, a stained glass window and original wallpaper from Europe. Throughout the home you will find antiques and original light fixtures. All four guest rooms offer queen size beds. The Prairie Room has its own private bath. The Heritage Room has a sink and shares a bath with the Kansas and Menno Haus rooms. Located 3 blocks from downtown shopping and a bike path along Sand Creek. Newton offers unique shopping, historical attractions, ethnic foods and small town friendliness.

Rates: $$ Includes full breakfast. No pets or smoking, please. We accept MasterCard and Visa.

Our guests love the different flavor.

Pumpkin Spice Pancakes

2 cups buttermilk pancake mix
1 1/3 cups milk
1/2 cup canned pumpkin
1/4 cup cooking oil
1 tablespoon sugar
1 teaspoon pumpkin pie spice
2 eggs

Heat griddle to 400°, grease lightly with oil. In medium bowl, combine all ingredients, stir just until ingredients are moistened. For each pancake, pour 1/4 cup batter into hot skillet. Cook 1 - 1 1/2 minutes, turning when edges look cooked and bubbles begin to break on surface. Cook 1 - 1 1/2 minutes more.

Makes 14 - 16 - 4" pancakes.

Heart Haven Inn

2145 Road 64 • Goodland, KS 67735
(913) 899-5171
Hosts: Cecil and Carol Bowen

Guests will experience a piece of history and country living at its finest when visiting Heart Haven Inn, the five acre bed and breakfast estate, located in the heart of the western KS wheat farming and ranching region. Enjoy a beautiful sunset while strolling the grounds or find a treasure while browsing in one of two shops located on the grounds, the Coo-Coo's Nest and the Book Bin. Relax in one of three common rooms provided for our guests' comfort, and help yourselves to dessert and coffee. The hosts are happy to share information about things to see in the area and have brochures available concerning some of the more interesting sights, such as the Kidder Massacre, the High Plains Museum, and a walking or driving tour of historic Goodland.

Rates: $ Includes full breakfast. Children are welcome. No pets or smoking, please.

Carol's grandmother's recipe is quite a bit different than others. She always said if someone didn't like mincemeat, they should try hers! It smells wonderful when cooking.

Grandma's Mincemeat Pie

1 cup hamburger
1 cup water
1 teaspoon salt
3 cups apples, peeled & chopped
1 cup raisins
1 cup cranberries or sour cherries
1 cup sugar
1 tablespoon cinnamon
1 teaspoon cloves
1/2 cup vinegar
Pastry for 2 double-crust pies

Simmer first three ingredients until meat is cooked. Add apples, raisins, cranberries, sugar, cinnamon, cloves and vinegar. Cook together for forty minutes. Place half of mincemeat mixture in each of two pastry-lined 9" pie plates. Place top pastry layers on each pie and flute edges. Cut slits in top layers or poke with a fork. Bake at 375° for 35 minutes or until crust is golden.

Makes 2 - 9" pies.

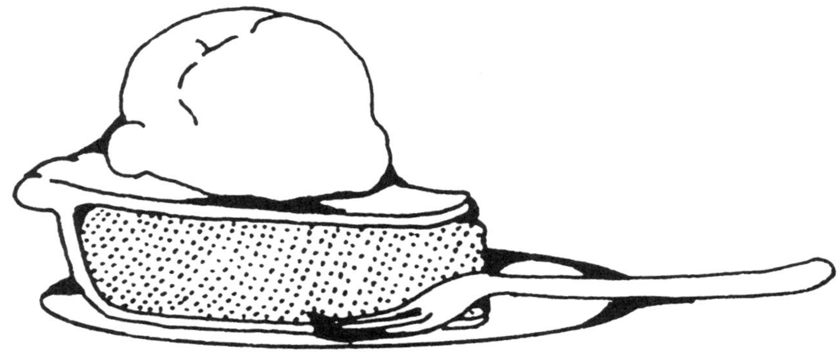

HEDGEAPPLE ACRES

HedgeApple Acres Bed & Breakfast, Inc.

R.R. #2, Box 27 • Moran, KS 66755
(316) 237-4646
Hosts: Jack and Ann Donaldson

With life becoming more and more hectic these days, it's no wonder folks enjoy escaping for a night or two to a place where old-fashioned values and timetables are still observed. The best in comfortable country living with just the right mix of hospitality and personal attention. Six guest rooms, with private baths. Enjoy casting a fishing line in our two stocked ponds, or a peaceful stroll around our more than 80 acres of beautifully preserved grounds. In the morning wake to a satisfying country breakfast with homemade bread and jelly. We use fresh garden vegetables in season. Near Historic Fort Scott and other scenic and recreational attractions.

Rates: $$ Includes country supper and full breakfast. Children are welcome. No pets or smoking, please. We accept MasterCard, Visa and Discover.

Meatballs and Red Gravy

1 lb. hamburger
2 eggs
12 oz. can tomato sauce
Crackers to taste
1/4 cup chopped onions (opt.)
1 1/2 cups cooked white rice (opt.)
Flour and water for gravy

Mix hamburger, eggs, 1/2 can tomato sauce, onions and rice (if desired) in large bowl. Crumble enough crackers to dry up meat mixture, so that meatballs can be formed which stick together nicely. Brown meatballs in large skillet. Remove meatballs, and add remainder of tomato sauce and flour to drippings. Add water to make gravy. Place meatballs back in gravy and simmer until meatballs are fully cooked. Serve over mashed potatoes.

Makes 4 - 6 servings.

The Holiday House Residential Bed & Breakfast

8406 W. Maple • Wichita, KS 67209
(316) 721-1968
Hosts: Diane and Carroll Parrett

Our home was begun in 1883, in 1950 it was finished to become a restaurant called THE FARM. It is almost 6,000 sq. ft. on 2 wooded acres, 5 minutes from Wichita's Mid-Continent Airport. We feature two guest rooms, one with queen canopy bed and the other with a king canopy bed. "The Dixie Lee Suite", is 16' x 23', has an antique sofa, private stairs, large bath, and an open balcony with domed rotunda ceiling that has displays of vintage clothing, wedding items, theatrical memorabilia, and old photos. The smaller room is "The Wichtanna" and has an old-fashioned sitting porch. Breakfast is served by candlelight either in room or downstairs. You receive a fresh rose, a treat basket of fruit/cookies/mints, and your choice of satin, cotton or flannel sheets. We prepare personalized banners to greet guests celebrating special occasions. We feature original MURDER MYSTERY NIGHTS on selected Saturday nights.

Rates: $$ - $$$ Includes full or continental plus breakfast. Children over 12 are welcome. No pets or smoking, please. We accept MasterCard and Visa.

Sweetheart's Casseroles

1/2 cup refrigerated loose-pack
hash brown potatoes
1/2 cup shredded Monterey Jack cheese
1/2 cup shredded mozzarella cheese
2 eggs
1/2 cup half and half

Preheat oven to 400°. Spray a little cooking oil in bottom of 2 - 8 oz. Pyrex casserole dishes. Line each with 1/4 cup of hash browns and bake uncovered for 20 minutes, or until golden brown. Reduce temperature to 350°, remove casseroles and let cool slightly. Sprinkle cheese evenly over each casserole (use all of cheese). Whisk eggs and half and half together. Divide evenly and pour over cheese/hash brown combination. Bake uncovered at 350° for about 25 minutes or until center appears set. Let stand 5 minutes before serving.

Makes 2 servings.

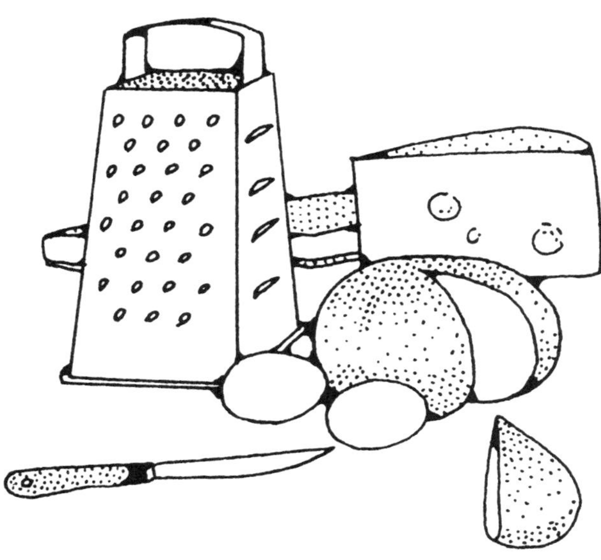

Huntington House

324 S. Main Street • Ft. Scott, KS 66701
(316) 223-3644 or (800) STAY-324
Hosts: Jeannie Volker and Wendy McDonald

Hospitality abounds at this Bed and Breakfast where you arrive as a guest and leave as a friend. Just a 5-minute walk from the Ft. Scott National Historic Site, this large brick home built in 1906 offers comfortable rooms, good food and an outdoor pool. The house was completely restored by family and friends and opened as a B&B in 1990. The outcome is an expansive living room and adjacent dining room decorated in hunter green trimmed in white, which shows off the exquisite leaded glass windows. Upstairs are four bedrooms, each with it's own unique decor and name. Hearts and Bows and Jamie's Garden each have a private bath. Captain's Quarters and Windsor Blue share the main bathroom. Antiques, handwork and Alaskan art are scattered throughout the house for your enjoyment.

Rates: $$ Includes full breakfast. Children are welcome. No smoking. We accept MasterCard and Visa.

Italian Quiche

Double crust for 9" pie
4 oz. bulk Italian sausage, browned and drained
3 eggs
1 cup ricotta or cream-style cottage cheese
4 oz. mozzarella cheese
1/2 cup sliced pepperoni, halved
1/2 cup fully cooked ham, cubed
1/4 cup grated Parmesan cheese
1 egg, beaten
Milk

Prepare 12" circle of pie crust and place into a 9" pie plate. Do not prick crust. Bake at 450° for 5 minutes. Set aside remaining pastry for top of quiche. Brown sausage and drain fat. Beat together eggs and ricotta or cottage cheese. Fold in remaining ingredients and turn into pastry shell. On lightly floured pastry sheet, roll remaining pastry dough into an 8" circle; cut into 6 wedges. Arrange wedges atop filling. Bake at 350° for 20 minutes. Combine beaten egg and milk, brush over wedges. Bake about 20 minutes more or until golden brown. Let stand 10 minutes before serving. Optional: May spoon Ragu spaghetti sauce over each serving.

Makes 4 - 6 servings.

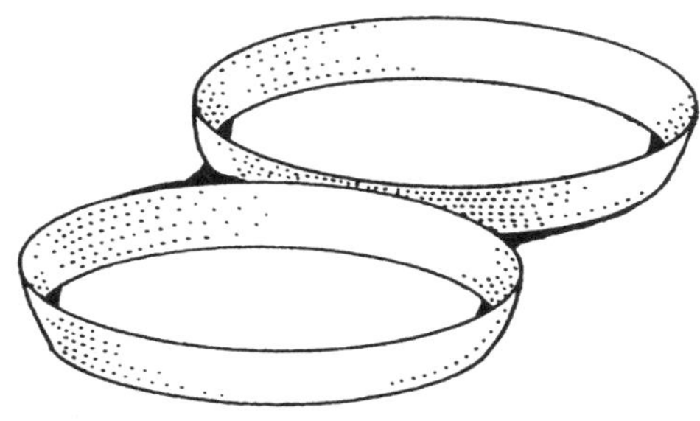

Inn at the Park

3751 E. Douglas • Wichita, KS 67218
(316) 652-0500 or (800) 258-1951
Hostess: Michelle Hickman

Built in 1909 by Mr. and Mrs. Cyrus M. Beachy in the fashionable College Hill area, at the turn-around point of the street car line and near the Wichita Country Club, the home remained a family residence until 1955. Mr. Beachy was chairman of the board and general manager of the Steffen Ice and Ice Cream Company, while Mrs. Beachy collected fine furniture, glassware, prints, and dolls. Today the three-story brick mansion enjoys a new life as The Inn at the Park. We are the perfect site, mid-week, for business travelers or small business meetings, and on weekends we welcome couples looking for that special romantic hideaway. Each morning we serve a complimentary continental breakfast that includes fresh baked breads and muffins, fresh fruits and juices, and other treats. Whether you wish to relax in the hot tub or work before a roaring fire, we provide the right setting for all your needs.

Rates: $$$ - $$$$ Includes continental plus breakfast. Children are welcome. No pets or smoking, please. We accept MasterCard, Visa, Am Ex and Discover.

Cinnamon Sour Cream Coffee Cake

1 cup butter
2 cups sugar
2 cups flour
1 teaspoon baking powder
1/4 teaspoon salt
3 eggs
1 teaspoon vanilla
8 oz. sour cream

Filling:
1 cup chopped pecans
2 teaspoons cinnamon
3 tablespoons brown sugar

Preheat oven to 325°. Cream butter and sugar. Sift dry ingredients and add to mixture, alternating with eggs. Mix batter thoroughly at slow speed of mixer. Add vanilla and sour cream. Pour half of batter into well-greased bundt pan. Mix filling ingredients together. Add half of filling over batter in pan. Pour remainder of batter over filling in pan, and top with remainder of filling mixture. Bake 65 - 70 minutes.

Makes 16 - 20 servings.

The Inn at Willowbend

3939 Comotara • Wichita, KS 67226
(316) 636-4032
Hosts: Gary and Bernice Adamson

The inn is situated adjacent to the No. 2 fairway on The Willowbend Golf Course. All rooms are named after golf courses. We have the feel of a B&B, with the amenities of a luxury hotel. Whether on business, a golf outing, or just a getaway, you'll love our hot breakfasts, cocktail hour, and cookie on your pillow. Reservations with credit card or prepayment only. 24 hour cancellation notice required.

Rates: $$$ - $$$$ Includes full breakfast. Children are welcome. No pets, please. Smoking allowed. We accept MasterCard, Visa, AmEx and Discover.

Eggs Willowbend

1 dozen eggs
1/4 cup sour cream
3/4 cup grated Cheddar cheese
1/4 cup salsa
20 slices of Canadian bacon
10 English muffins
1 1/2 cups Hollandaise sauce
10 cantaloupe slices
10 small blueberry muffins

Line 12" x 18" baking sheet with buttered parchment baker's paper turned up on all four sides, so egg mixture will not run underneath. Blend eggs and sour cream until smooth, pour into lined baking pan. Bake in preheated 350° oven for 15 minutes or until firm. Remove from oven, sprinkle cheese evenly over eggs. Place salsa along one short end of the eggs. Starting with that end roll the eggs into a tight roll like a jelly roll. Grill English muffins and warm the bacon. Place two muffin halves on the plate. Top first with bacon, then a slice of the egg roll. Cover with Hollandaise sauce. Place a small blueberry muffin and cantaloupe slice on the plate to make a Happy Face.

Makes 10 servings.

THE IRON GATE INN
Bed and Breakfast

The Iron Gate Inn

1203 E. 9th • Winfield, KS 67156
(316) 221-7202
Hosts: Donna and Larry Markley

The Iron Gate Inn was built circa 1885 by John Peter Baden for his wife and two sons. He was a prominent businessman, philanthropist, and one of Winfield's most illustrious citizens. This grand Victorian, white-pillared home is a familiar landmark to Winfield residents and is still referred to as "The Baden House". The house is full of interesting and original decorating items. Floors are of handmade parquet and oak. The staircase is of handcarved walnut. Light fixtures in the dining room and bedroom have retractable fan blades. There are 3 working fireplaces to warm guests on a cold winter's night. Five guest bedrooms with private baths, TV, a/c, and steam heat are uniquely decorated. A full country breakfast is served.

Rates: $$ Includes full breakfast. No pets or smoking, please. We accept MasterCard and Visa.

Cherry-Pineapple Crepes

21 oz. can cherry pie filliing
8 oz. can chunk pineapple, well-drained
1/8 teaspoon almond extract
6 crepes (use very thin pancake mixture)
Sour cream to taste
Brown sugar to taste

For crepes: Heat small skillet. Spray pan with non-stick spray. Pour 1/3 cup of thin pancake mixture of your choice into skillet. Swirl skillet to cover entire bottom with mixture. Cook only one side of crepe. Put filling on the uncooked side of the crepe. For filling: Combine cherry pie filling, pineapple and almond extract in saucepan. Heat through over medium heat. Place crepe on a hot serving plate. Spoon a little of the hot filling down the center of each crepe. Fold up sides. Spoon a dollop of sour cream on each crepe. Sprinkle with brown sugar. Serve immediately.

Makes 4 - 6 servings.

Kimble Cliff

6782 Anderson Ave. • Manhattan, KS 66502
(913) 539-3816
Hosts: Betty and Neil Anderson

Kimble Cliff was built in 1894 as a farm home, of limestone quarried nearby, hand-fashioned and decorated. It has 10 rooms and a full attic, fruit cellar, storm cellar and ice house. Two of the bedrooms are used for bed & breakfast, and they share a bath. The home is well-endowed with antiques collected by the owners and there is an antique business in the stone barn on the property, managed by Betty. Neil is a professor at Kansas State University, and also has a sheep flock protected by a llama. We are closed the months of July and August each year.

Rates: $ Includes continental plus breakfast. Children are welcome. No pets or smoking, please.

This recipe was found in Good Housekeeping magazine. Tried and tested by husband, 6 children, and 8 grandchildren!

Peanut Butter Muffins

1 3/4 cups flour
1/2 cup sugar
1 tablespoon baking powder
3/4 cup milk
1/2 cup crunchy peanut butter
1/3 cup oil
1 egg
1/2 cup raisins

In large bowl mix flour, sugar and baking powder. In medium bowl mix milk, peanut butter, oil and egg. Stir this into flour mixture until moistened. Do not overmix or muffins will be tough. Batter should be lumpy. Add raisins. Spoon batter into prepared muffin pan. Bake at 400° for 20 minutes.

Makes 8 - 12 muffins.

Kirk House

145 West 4th Avenue • Garnett, KS 66032-1313
(913) 448-5813
Hosts: Robert Cugno, Robert Logan, Angie Williams

This Neoclassic Revival was designed in 1913 by George Washburn, prominent KS architect. The exterior boasts a green glazed tile roof and a porch with classic columns. Kirk House has 23 rooms on four levels, with five bedrooms available to guests. Though large it is, the house is invitingly comfortable and homey. Features include Tiger-grained woodwork, Tiffany glass tile fireplace, leaded glass cabinets, a mural which surrounds the dining room, and a Rookwood tile fireplace. Landscaping, which has something blooming during any season, features native perennials, ornamental grasses, shrubs and trees. A fish pond highlights the rear garden. A wildflower/prairie grass garden complements a grove of dwarf fruit trees. Your hosts: art dealers, interior designers, social & event planners, community-minded individuals who arrived in KS from CA in 1988. The entire house is open for guests to enjoy viewing the owners' collections.

Rates: $ - $$ Includes full breakfast. No children, pets, or smoking, please. We accept MasterCard and Visa.

Spicy Coffee Cake

2 1/4 cups flour
1/2 teaspoon salt
2 teaspoons cinnamon
1/4 teaspoon ginger
1 cup brown sugar
3/4 cup white sugar
3/4 cup corn oil
1 cup chopped walnuts
1 teaspoon baking soda
1 teaspoon baking powder
1 egg, beaten
1 cup buttermilk

Mix together flour, salt, 1 teaspoon cinnamon, ginger, both sugars and corn oil. Remove 3/4 cup of this mixture, and add it to the remaining 1 teaspoon cinnamon and walnuts. Mix this well and set aside. To flour mixture add baking soda, baking powder, egg, and buttermilk. Mix to combine; there may be small lumps in batter. Pour batter into well greased 9" x 13" x 2" pan. Sprinkle reserved mixture evenly over the surface. Bake at 350° for 40 - 45 minutes.

Makes 12 servings.

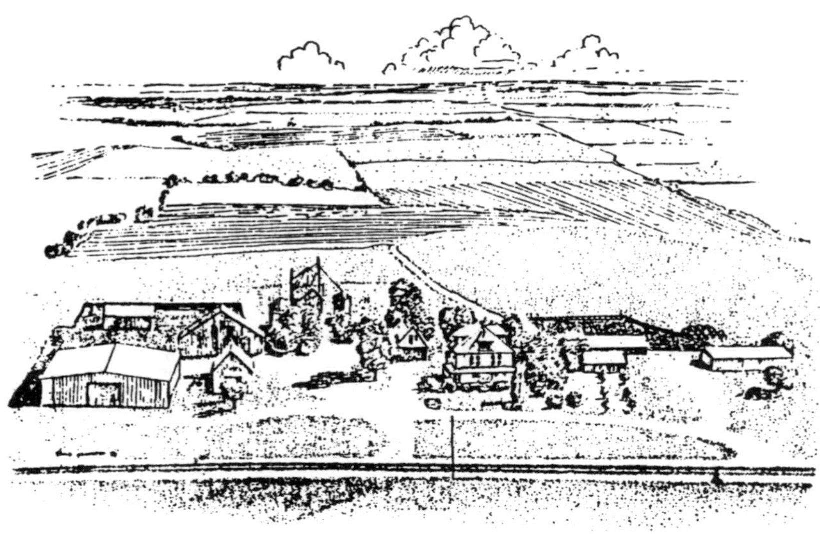

Lear Acres

Route 1, Box 31 • Bern, KS 66408-9715
(913) 336-3903
Hosts: Byron and Toby Lear

If a change of pace has appeal for you, a warm country welcome awaits you at our farm. The 2-story house was built by Byron's father for his new bride in 1918. Much of the furnishings are from that era, including the bed where Byron was born. Some of the furniture was that of Byron's grandparents, who were early homesteaders in this Swiss community. Byron farms 760 acres of diversified crops and also manages hog and beef cattle operations. Toby and the farm animals will do all they can to make your visit homey and comfortable. We proudly serve a full farm breakfast made from meats, eggs, wheat and fruits all home-raised. Come sit in our porch swing and enjoy the "quiet" sounds. Visit Pony Express and Oregon Trail sights. Or perhaps hunt for antiques, game or historical finds.

Rates: $ Includes full/continental plus breakfast. Children welcome with adult supervision. Outside pets only. Restricted smoking.

Leftovers are good!

Rio Grande Pork Roast

4 - 5 lb. pork roast (boneless preferred)
1/2 teaspoon salt
1/2 teaspoon garlic salt
1/2 teaspoon chili powder
1/2 cup apple jelly
1/2 cup catsup
1 tablespoon vinegar
1/2 teaspoon chili powder
1 cup crushed corn chips

Place pork in shallow roasting pan. Combine garlic salt, salt and 1/2 teaspoon chili powder. Rub into roast. Roast at 325° for 2 - 2 1/2 hours. In saucepan combine jelly, catsup, vinegar and 1/2 teaspoon chili powder. Bring to a boil, then simmer 2 minutes. Brush roast with this glaze. Sprinkle on corn chips and continue cooking 10 - 15 minutes until roast is done. Remove from oven and let stand 10 minutes. Measure drippings and chips that have fallen and add water to make 1 cup. Bring this sauce to a boil and pass with meat.

Makes 7 - 10 servings.

The Loft Bed & Breakfast

520 N. First • Osborne, KS 67473
(913) 346-5984
Hosts: Russell and Irene Phalen

Our two guest rooms on the second floor are furnished with family pieces of a pre-30's era. Our queen beds boast of comfortable mattresses. The large bath with double sinks and mirrors, and tub/shower gives lots of room. The guest rooms share a common sitting room with lots of reading material. Guests may watch TV in the living room or join us in the kitchen. We love to meet new people and share our home. We are less than a block from the walking track and swimming pool. Other recreation nearby. We take pictures of our guests for our growing "family guest" album.

Rates: $ Includes full breakfast. Children are welcome. No pets or smoking, please.

These muffins may be frozen and/or reheated in microwave oven.

Blueberry Muffins

1/2 cup margarine or shortening
3/4 cup sugar
2 eggs
1 teaspoon vanilla
2 cups flour
1/4 teaspoon salt
2 teaspoons baking powder
1/4 cup milk
16 1/2 oz. can blueberries, well-drained

Beat shortening until fluffy. Add sugar and beat again. Add eggs and vanilla, and beat again. Stir in sifted dry ingredients alternately with milk. Carefully fold in drained blueberries. Bake in greased muffin tins at 375° for 20 - 25 minutes. May use 2 cups fresh or frozen berries, but increase sugar by 1/4 cup. For added touch, mix chopped walnuts with a bit of sugar and sprinkle on top of muffins before baking.

Makes 18 muffins.

Meriwether House Bed & Breakfast

322 W. Pine Street • Columbus, KS 66725
(316) 429-2812
Hostess: Margaret Meriwether

Visit our cottage on your next trip through southeast KS. Lovingly restored, our little green house on Pine Street is filled with antiques, lace, and accessories. Located just 2 hours from Kansas City, Branson and Tulsa, we offer 4 bedrooms with private baths, 2 sitting rooms and kitchen. You will enjoy the peaceful relaxation only a small town bed & breakfast can offer.

Rates: $ Includes continental breakfast. Children are welcome. No pets or smoking, please. We accept MasterCard, Visa, and Discover.

Peanut Butter Swirl Bars

1/2 cup crunchy peanut butter
1/3 cup softened butter
3/4 cup firmly packed brown sugar
3/4 cup granulated sugar
2 eggs
2 teaspoons vanilla
1 cup flour
1 teaspoon baking powder
1/4 teaspoon salt
12 oz. pkg. chocolate chips

In large bowl cream peanut butter, butter, brown sugar and granulated sugar. Add eggs and vanilla. Add dry ingredients. Spread into greased 9" x 13" pan and sprinkle with chocolate chips. Bake at 350° for 5 minutes. Run knife through to swirl chocolate, and bake an additional 30 minutes.

Makes 24 bars.

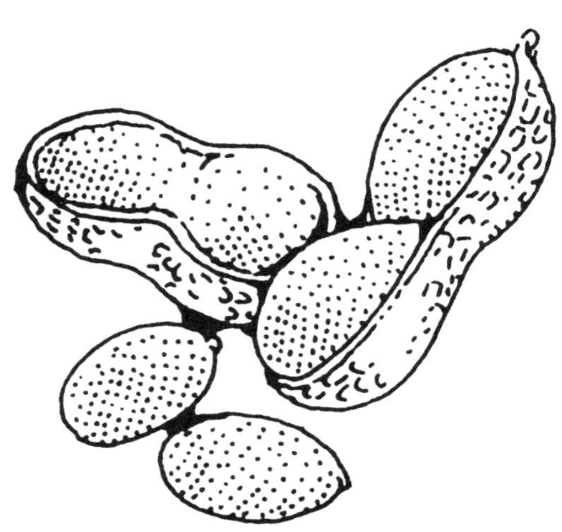

The Moore-Ballard Inn

301 W. 2nd • Washington, KS 66968
(913) 325-3292
Hosts: Dave and Beth Dunham

Experience history on the Oregon Trail in a country setting with a touch of Victorian flavor. Located within 25 miles of three Pony Express Stations, the Moore-Ballard Inn is a recently renovated Italianate style Victorian house built in 1878 by A. W. Moore, a prominent Washington, KS businessman. In 1901, Moore sold the home to Civil War captain David E. Ballard. Ballard was instrumental in the settling of Washington County and establishing the city of Washington. Enjoy sipping iced tea on the wraparound porch, curling up with a good book in the window seat, or relaxing in the bedroom furnished with period antiques. Wake up to the aroma of breakfast being prepared specially for you!

Rates: $ Includes full breakfast. Children are welcome. Pets allowed, boarding available. No smoking. We accept MasterCard and Visa.

Dave does 1840's "Mountain Man" reenactments and demonstrations, and this is a favorite at the rendezvous!

Beef or Deer Jerky

5 lbs. very lean beef or deer meat
1 cup K.C. Masterpiece hickory barbeque sauce
1/2 cup Worcestershire sauce
1/4 cup soy sauce
1/2 cup hot water
1 tablespoon liquid smoke
1 tablespoon onion salt
1 tablespoon garlic salt

Cut meat into strips 1/4" thick. Mix all ingredients except meat in a large bowl. Blend, if necessary, to distribute the salts. Criss-cross the strips of meat in layers in the marinade sauce. Let it marinate overnight, occasionally stirring to redistribute the sauce. Place meat in single layers on dehydrator racks at about 180°. Rotate racks at 2-hour intervals and remove strips individually as they become dry, but not brittle. Note: An oven can be used at it's lowest setting with door propped open a few inches.

Yield: LOTS!!!

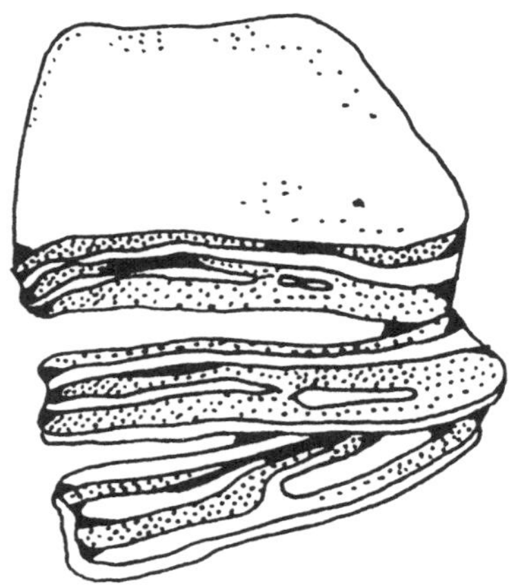

nee Murray way Bed & Breakfast

220 W. Third • Halstead, KS 67056
(316) 835-2027
Hosts: Gary, Dru and Kathelyn Wranosky

As you come up the front walk of this enchanting Victorian house built in 1911, you'll notice the tree-laden lawn with over 30 different varieties of trees from all over the world. Enter through the lovely foyer, complete with original leaded and beveled glass, and you will be swept back to the turn of the century. Our guest rooms have queen beds, and offer a quiet solitude and feel of times gone by. Within walking distance to downtown and antiques, gift shops and a basketier. Main Street is still paved with bricks and it's easy to picture the old carriages moving to and fro. Near the first home of Bernhard Warkentin, a forefather of Halstead, the Kit Carson tree in Riverside Park, and the Kansas Learning Center for Health.

Rates: $ - $$ Includes full breakfast. Children are welcome.
No pets or smoking, please.

Perfect Loaf Bread

1 1/2 cups milk
1 cup water
1/4 cup sugar
1 tablespoon salt
2 heaping tablespoons Crisco
2 packages dry yeast
1 teaspoon baking powder
Approximately 8 cups flour

Heat milk and water; scald, do not boil. Add sugar, salt and shortening. Let cool. Add yeast and baking powder, mix well. Work in flour until elastic and satiny. Let rise to double, punch down. Let rise to double again, punch down. Work dough with oil on hands. Place in oiled loaf pans. Let rise to double a third time. Bake at 325° until golden brown.

Makes 3 loaves.

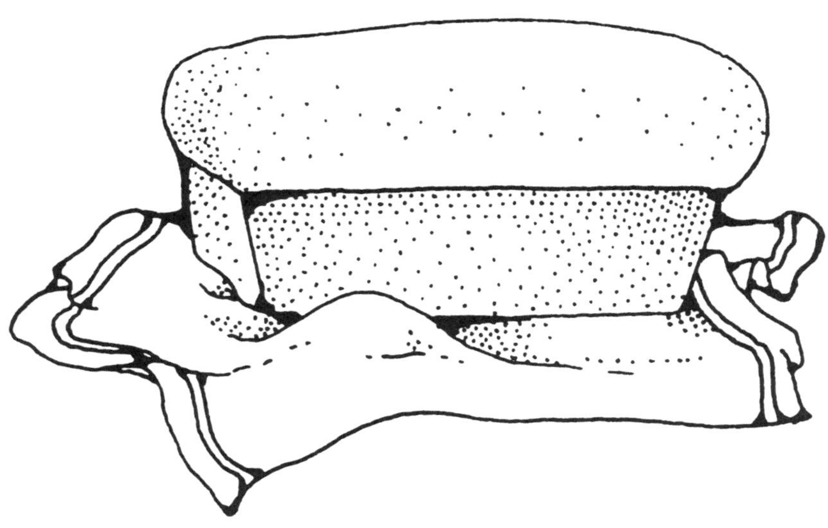

A Nostalgic Bed-Breakfast Place

310 S. Main • Hillsboro, KS 67063
(316) 947-3519
Hosts: Don and Mildred Harding

Located in a small farming community in south central KS, with a population of 2,800. Near Tabor College, hospital, golf course, lovely city park, Abode house and museum, churches and restaurants. The home was built in 1915 and remains much as it was then, decorated in original country! Two rooms are available, upstairs on second floor, each with full bed and sharing a bath. Both rooms have ceiling fans, one has a/c. Sitting room with mini-museum, old books, reading material, and a radio also on second floor. This room has windows on three sides with a view of trees and homes. Enjoy downstairs TV with the family. Some handmade items are available to purchase, if desired. Full breakfast is served before 8:30 A.M. Dinner available upon request.

Rates: $ Includes full breakfast. Children over 16 are welcome. No pets or smoking, please. We accept cash or personal checks only.

Quiche Lorraine

9" baked pie shell
8 slices bacon, cooked crisply, drained & crumbled
1 cup shredded Swiss cheese
6 eggs
1 1/4 cups milk or half & half
1/2 teaspoon salt
1/8 teaspoon ground nutmeg
1/8 teaspoon pepper

Preheat oven to 375°. Sprinkle crumbled bacon and cheese into baked pie shell. Beat together remaining ingredients until well blended. Pour over bacon and cheese. Bake 30 - 40 minutes until knife inserted near center comes out clean. Let stand 5 minutes before serving.

Makes 6 servings.

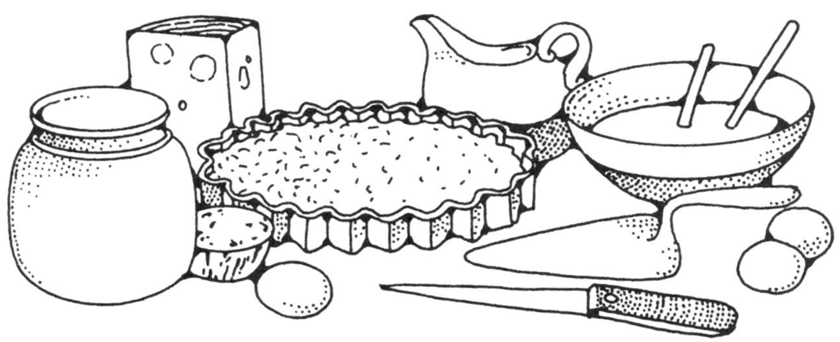

Old Glory Guest House

600 N. Spruce • Abilene, KS 67410
(913) 263-3225
Hosts: Linda and Sam Hawes

Old Glory Guest House is conveniently located only 2 miles south of I-70 in a quiet, residential neighborhood just around the corner from downtown Abilene. In this town of historic mansions, museums and antique/craft shops, this late 1800's Italianate-style home features tall ceilings, elegant woodwork, pocket doors and a wraparound back porch. The "Five Star Guestroom" honoring Abilene native Dwight D. Eisenhower, is furnished with a full-sized antique bed with matching furniture and a modern private bath. A collection of books, magazines, and newspapers celebrating the Eisenhower years is complemented by the family's own collection of family military memorabilia. Breakfast may be served in the sunny bay-windowed dining room or in the privacy of the guest room. Your choice of a full or light breakfast may be of Eggs Benedict, French toast, omelets or homemade biscuits.

Rates: $$ Includes full or continental breakfast. Children over 6 are welcome. No pets, but boarding arrangements can be made. No smoking.

Sam's grandmother always brings this when she visits, and when we visit her, we expect one!

Grandmama's Chocolate Cake

1/2 cup buttermilk
1 teaspoon baking soda
2 cups flour
2 cups sugar
1 stick oleo or butter
1/2 cup shortening
4 tablespoons cocoa
1 cup water
2 eggs
1 teaspoon vanilla
1 teaspoon cinnamon

Frosting:
4 tablespoons cocoa
6 tablespoons Pet evaporated milk
1 stick oleo or butter
1 lb. box sifted confectioners sugar
1 teaspoon vanilla

Mix buttermilk and soda well, and set aside. Sift flour and sugar into bowl, set aside. Put oleo or butter, shortening, cocoa and water into saucepan, bring to rapid boil. Pour over flour/sugar mixture and mix well. Add buttermilk mixture, eggs, vanilla and cinnamon. Mix well. Pour into greased and floured 9" x 13" oblong pan. Bake at 400° for 30 minutes. For frosting: Bring cocoa, milk, and oleo to a hard boil. Add confectioners sugar and vanilla. Pour over still warm cake.

Makes 1 - 9" x 13" cake.

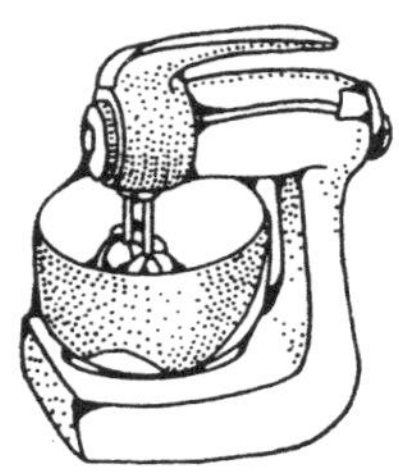

Peaceful Acres Bed & Breakfast

Route 5, Box 153 • Great Bend, KS 67530
(316) 793-7527
Hosts: Dale and Doris Nitzel

We are a mini-farm with a sprawling old farmhouse, and two large rooms with a shared bath. If more than one set of guests occupy the house, they would share the bath. There is a working windmill, small livestock, chickens and guineas, dog and cats. A rock wall around the yard and lots of trees add to the comfort. Your complimentary breakfast will consist of homemade hot breads, fresh eggs, juice, hot coffee or tea, milk and cereal if desired. All you can eat! Most is home-grown. Close to Cheyenne Bottoms, Lindsborg, Pawnee Rock, Santa Fe Trail, Dodge City, Wilson Lake, and Ft. Larned.

Rates: $ Includes full breakfast. Children are welcome. Pets allowed. No smoking, please. We accept personal checks.

This dish came from our daughter-in-law, and is very good.

Pork One-Dish Meal

1 lb. ground pork,
browned and drained
1 1/2 cups cooked macaroni
1 can cream of chicken soup
3 - 4 oz. can evaporated milk
1 cup diced American cheese
1 cup seasoned croutons

Brown and drain pork. Mix together all ingredients except croutons, and place in greased 2 quart casserole. Top with croutons. Bake at 350° for 30 minutes.

Makes 4 - 6 servings.

Plumb House B&B

628 Exchange • Emporia, KS 66801
(316) 342-6881
Hostess: Barbara Stoecklein

This 1910 Mission era home built by George and Ellen Plumb is situated in downtown Emporia, just one block from Hwy. 50. The large front porch invites you to come "sit a spell" and to step back in time to enjoy Victorian elegance in beveled glass windows, pocket doors, a beautiful oak stairway, and antique furnishings in a peaceful setting. The guest rooms are: The Garden Suite, Horseless Carriage, Rosalie, and Victoriana, each one decorated to please the eye and give comfort with private bathrooms and queen beds. Tea party guests are served an elegant tea in the dining room, and then climb to Grannie's Attic for a delightful dress-up time, including beautiful hats, long dresses, gloves, pearls, purses and shoes.

Rates: $ - $$ Includes full breakfast. Children are welcome. No pets, please.

An English toast to a person's health, from the past, but equally enjoyed today.

Hot Wassail

1 quart hot tea
1 quart cranberry juice
1 quart apple juice
2 cups orange juice
3/4 cup lemon juice
1 cup sugar
12 cloves
3 pieces cinnamon stick

Combine all ingredients and simmer to enhance the flavor. Serve hot for Christmas holiday parties, or anytime the weather's chilly!

Makes 25 servings.

Pomeroy Inn

224 W. Main • Hill City, KS 67642
(913) 674-2098
Hosts: Don and Mary Worcester

Our building is over 107 years old; it's two story, so far we only use the lower floor. But we are continually striving to fix up and get to it this fall - a new sidewalk on the west side is in the planning stages now. We have 8 - 9 rooms downstairs which are very quiet and comfortable. Each is decorated differently. Mary works a full-time job besides running the Inn. The kids also help us out with cleaning and repairs. Enjoy Mary's special whole-wheat rolls every morning.

Rates: $ Includes continental plus breakfast. Pets and smoking allowed. We accept MasterCard, Visa, Discover and Diner's.

Swedish Ice Box Cookies

3 cups sifted flour
1 teaspoon baking soda
1 1/2 teaspoons salt
1 teaspoon cinnamon
1/2 teaspoon nutmeg
1 cup shortening
2 cups brown sugar
2 eggs
2 - 3 teaspoons vanilla flavoring

Sift flour, soda, salt, and spices together. Set aside. Work shortening until soft. Gradually add brown sugar and blend thoroughly. Add unbeaten eggs with vanilla to shortening mixture. Gradually add flour. Turn soft dough onto floured waxed paper. Shape into 4 rolls, and chill overnight (24 hours) in refrigerator. (This dough can be stored up to a week in fridge). Cut cookies 1/8" - 1/4" thick. Bake on greased cookie sheet at 375° about 10 minutes or until golden brown.

Queen Anne's Lace Bed & Breakfast

2617 Queen Anne's Lace • Rose Hill, KS 67133
(316) 733-4075
Hosts: Jackie and Bob Collison

Envision a peaceful country setting with windswept days and starlit evenings in relaxing, comfortable surroundings. You will enjoy a lovely modern home located on five wooded acres at the southeastern edge of Wichita. A stay in either charming bedroom includes a full size bed, private bath, and common area for guests with TV, VCR, fireplace, while just outside on the patio is a hot tub. Full breakfasts feature Bob's special pancakes or Jackie's Stuffed French Toast, with fresh fruit salad, breakfast meat, very fresh eggs and our special selection of freshly ground coffee. Queen Anne's Lace is especially convenient to most east-side shops and PKD Arena with easy access to local aircraft factories, the KS Turnpike and I-35 Highway. You may "visit" with the horses and goats, dogs and cats, or take a relaxing stroll along the wooded creek. Whatever your preference, you will feel a sense of comfort and serenity in this homestay B&B.

Rates: $ - $$ 10% discount for senior citizens. Includes full breakfast. Well-behaved children are welcome. Well-controlled pets allowed. No smoking.

With lots of goat's milk and homemade bread, this recipe just "grew" out of our kitchen!

Stuffed French Toast by Jackie

3 eggs
3/4 cup milk (goat's milk is best)
Dash of cinnamon
1 tablespoon orange zest
12 slices raisin bread
6 - 10 oz. cream cheese
4 tablespoons butter

Beat eggs, then add milk, cinnamon, and orange zest, and beat a little more. Spread a generous tablespoon of cream cheese on 6 of the bread slices. Top each with another slice. Dip each "sandwich" into the batter, then fry in the melted butter until golden brown on each side. Serve hot with syrup or jam.

Makes 6 servings.

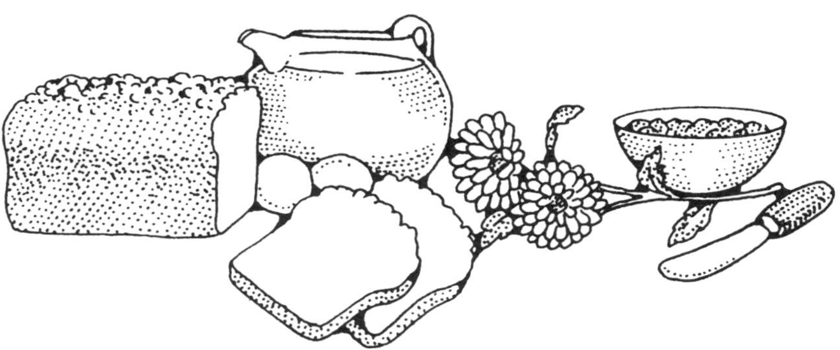

The Slaton House

319 W. 7th • Ashland, KS 67831
(316) 635-2290
Hosts: Curtis and Sally Slaton

The Slaton House offers a pleasant alternative from the motel or hotel scene. We have two guest rooms and our guests are encouraged to use the living room to socialize, watch TV, or to simply relax and read. The Slaton House features a "home away from home" atmosphere. We offer a full breakfast suited for the individual guest. Breakfast may be served from 6:30 A.M. to 9:00 A.M. Check-in after 3:00 P.M. and check-out by 10:00 A.M.

Rates: $ - $$ Includes full breakfast. Children are welcome. No pets or smoking, please.

Applesauce Muffins

1 egg
2 tablespoons oil
1 1/2 cups unsweetened applesauce
1 1/2 cups whole wheat flour
1/2 cup Bran Buds cereal
1/2 teaspoon baking soda
2 teaspoons baking powder
1/2 teaspoon nutmeg
1/2 teaspoon cinnamon
1/2 cup raisins

Mix egg, oil and applesauce in bowl. Add flour, Bran Buds, baking soda, baking powder and spices. Fold in raisins carefully. Spoon batter into nonstick or paper-lined muffin pan, 3/4 full. Bake at 400° for 20 - 25 minutes.

Makes 12 muffins.

Smoky Valley Bed & Breakfast

Second and State Streets • Lindsborg, KS 67456-2212
(913) 227-4460 or (800) 532-4407
Hosts: Signe Geist and Bill Molinski

Comfortable, red brick, century-old home set in an extensive garden area, the perfect getaway retreat from which to enjoy "Little Sweden", Lindsborg. All 3 rooms offer queen size bed, private bath, color cable TV, VCR and a/c. Each is a corner room, offering views of the flowers and grand old trees surrounding the house. The rooms share a private sitting room, perfect for curling up with a book or making morning coffee. Family heirlooms are used to make each room distinct. Located just a block from downtown stores, galleries, restaurants and art studios. Convenient to Bethany College, two museums and golfing. Our Swedish heritage is cherished in festivals throughout the year and in the character of Lindsborg's downtown. Come and enjoy our hospitality!

Rates: $ Includes full/continental breakfast. Children are welcome. No pets or smoking, please. We accept Visa and personal checks.

German Pancakes

4 eggs
1 1/2 cups milk
2 tablespoons sugar
Dash of salt
1 1/2 cups flour
1/2 teaspoon baking powder

Beat all ingredients together until foamy. Fry pancakes on hot, oiled griddle, using half cup of batter per pancake. Let batter run thin on griddle. Turn when light golden. Good with blueberries for topping.

Makes 8 pancakes.

Spruce House Bed & Breakfast

604 N. Spruce • Abilene, KS 67410
(913) 263-3900
Hosts: Victoria Page and Earl Levine

Spruce House is a 110 year old house with three guest rooms, all one flight up and all containing full private bath. We use only 100% cotton bed linens, so we spend a lot of time ironing!!! Fresh flowers always adorn every room, year-round. I am a vegetarian, (however, carnivores are very welcome) so we can readily serve unique full veggie breakfasts and can happily cater to guests with food allergies. We serve fabulous multi-grain homemade bread, and Earl makes superb fresh spinach, mushroom, pesto, or Denver omelets. Join us and bon appétit!

Rates: $ - $$ Includes full breakfast. Well-behaved children are welcome. Pets allowed with advance notice. No smoking.

We ate a dish similar to this at a sidewalk café in Greenwich Village in New York City. It's great for guests who are tired of eggs and pancakes!!!

Breakfast Pasta

3 oz. assorted pasta
Sausage or prosage to taste, cooked
and cut into bite-size pieces
Plain yogurt with active cultures
1 apple, cut into pieces
Crumbled walnuts, to taste
A handful of raisins
Cinnamon to taste
Dash of parsley, sage,
rosemary and thyme
Salt to taste
Crushed garlic (opt.)

Let yogurt come to room temperature. Cook pasta according to package directions, two different kinds make this dish look prettier. Cook sausage or prosage (textured sausage-flavored soy product available at health food stores), and cut into bite-size pieces. Wash and cut apples into bite-size shapes. Drain pasta and add a touch of olive oil to keep it from sticking. Add a bit of crushed garlic if desired. Stir in a healthy amount of yogurt, with a good bit of cinnamon and a dash of other spices listed. Salt to taste. Add apples, walnuts, raisins and sausage. Stir, put on plate and serve. Yum!

Makes 1 serving.

The Sunbarger

Route 1 • Cassoday, KS 66842
(316) 735-4499
Hosts: Dale and Judy Remsberg

Enjoy privacy and comfort of charming turn-of-the-century guest house set on spacious grounds, surrounded by wooded bluestem pasture, longhorn cattle, and quarter horses. Within a mile of Cassoday I-35 turnpike exit, real cowtown and gateway to scenic Flinthills. Catered meals to your taste. Breakfast features freshly baked homemade sweet rolls. Artists, antiques, cowboys abound!

Rates: $ Includes continental plus breakfast. No children or smoking, please. Horses are the only pets allowed. We accept personal checks (one-half payment confirms reservation).

Plum Dum, so named by middle sonflower, Tad, many years ago, is a wonderfully rich and versatile cobbler that dresses up or down with cream, ice cream, or whipped cream. Baked solo in a round pan, you have the base for the best shortcake! If there's a small dish remaining, reheat with cream. It's comfort food for breakfast. Original version called for fresh peaches and blueberries, but 3 cups of any fresh, frozen or canned fruit will work. Recipe doubles easily, bet you like it! M-m-m-m-m-m-m, good!

Plum Dum

Fruit:
1 tablespoon cornstarch
1/4 cup brown sugar
30 oz. can purple plums
1 tablespoon butter
1 tablespoon lemon juice

Cobbler:
1 cup sifted all-purpose flour
1/2 cup sugar
1 1/2 teaspoons baking powder
1/2 teaspoon salt
1/2 cup milk
1/4 cup soft butter

Topping:
2 tablespoons sugar
1/4 teaspoon freshly grated nutmeg

Mix first two ingredients. Add pitted plums and juice. Cook and stir until mixture thickens. Add 1 tablespoon butter and lemon juice. Pour into 8" x 8" x 2" ovenware. Sift dry ingredients for cobbler batter. Add milk and butter; beat until smooth. Pour over fruit. Sprinkle sugar and nutmeg over batter. Bake at 350° for 30 minutes.

Makes 6 servings.

The Sunflower Bed & Breakfast

915 S. W. Munson Avenue • Topeka, KS 66604
(913) 357-7509
Hosts: Bryan Eakes, Michael and Joan Stringer

The Sunflower is a Queen Anne Victorian home that was built in 1887. It is a KS landmark that has been restored to its original splendor. It received a 1991 Preservation Award from Historic Topeka, Inc. The home is located in the historic Holliday Park District, and due to its central location is minutes from many Topeka attractions, including the State Capitol Building, Heartland Park Raceway, the Topeka Performing Arts Center, the world famous Topeka Zoo, and the Kansas Expocentre. Every room is a designer's delight. Reproduction wallpapers and rich color schemes add to the nostalgic charm. Stained glass windows, Eastlake style fireplace mantels, plaster moldings, medallions, and an extensive collection of period furnishings and memorabilia all add to the home's Victorian character.

Rates: $ Includes full breakfast. Children are welcome. Pets allowed in carriers.

This is a quick, easy, and delicious breakfast or brunch dish that goes great with pancakes, muffins, etc.

Early Morning Omelette

2 tablespoons butter or margarine
7 eggs, beaten
1/4 teaspoon salt
1/3 cup sour cream
1/4 cup milk
1 cup diced ham or cooked
pork sausage
3/4 cup shredded Cheddar cheese

Preheat oven to 350°. Melt butter in a 9" x 9" glass baking dish. Whip eggs, add remaining ingredients and whip again. Pour into baking dish with butter. Bake for 40 - 45 minutes, until knife inserted in center comes out clean.

Makes 4 generous servings.

Thistle Hill Bed & Breakfast

Route 1, Box 93 • WaKeeney, KS 67672
(913) 743-2644
Hosts: Dave and Mary Hendricks

A comfortable, secluded, cedar farm home halfway between Kansas City and Denver along I-70. Experience farm life and visit Castle Rock. Walk through prairie wildflowers in the 60 acre prairie-wildlife restoration. Enjoy a hearty country breakfast, featuring fresh homemade muffins and hot cakes often made from freshly-ground KS wheat, by the fireplace or on the summer porch overlooking the flower and herb garden. The "Prairie Room" has a romantic, king size round bed and is decorated in honor of family members that were early pioneers of Trego County. The "Sunflower Room's" white iron bed is graced with a handmade KS Sunflower quilt. The best view of the working windmill is from the window of this room. Sleeping on the Jenny Lind bed in the "Wren's Nest" is almost like sleeping under the stars. The spacious "Oak Room" has a queen size bed.

Rates: $$ Includes full breakfast. Children are welcome. No pets or smoking, please.

This was a favorite combination of fruit used by my Grandmother Schneider because the rhubarb and mulberries were readily available on their farm. The sweetness of the mulberries and tartness of the rhubarb complement each other very well. You may substitute blueberries for mulberries, if you don't have a mulberry tree in your back yard!

Rhubarb Mulberry Pie

1 cup sugar
3 tablespoons all-purpose flour
1/8 teaspoon salt
2 cups cut rhubarb
1 1/2 cups mulberries
2 tablespoons butter
Pastry for 9" 2-crust pie

In small bowl, combine sugar, flour and salt. Mix well. In separate bowl, combine rhubarb and mulberries. Sprinkle sugar mixture over the fruit, mixing lightly. Line pie pan with half of the pastry. Fill pastry with rhubarb mixture, dot with butter and top with remaining pastry. Cut vents in the top crust and sprinkle with additional sugar. Bake at 450° for 10 minutes, then reduce heat to 350°, and bake for 35 minutes longer or until middle of pie is bubbly.

Makes 6 servings.

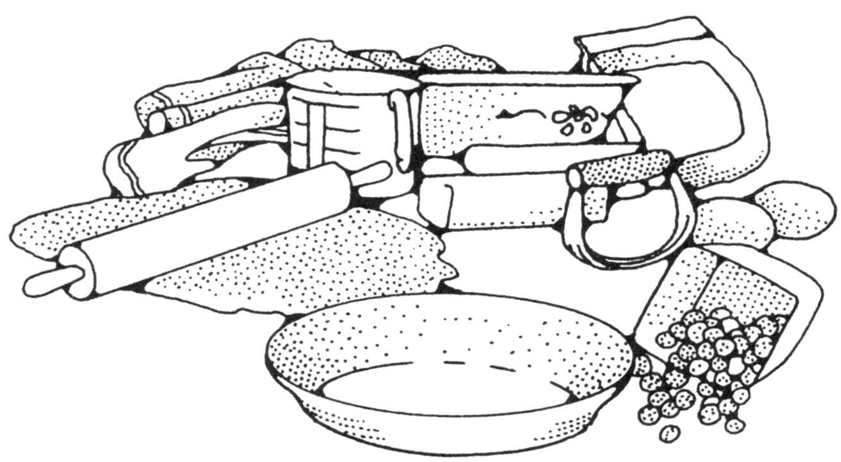

Trix's Riley Roomer

104 N. Hartner • Riley, KS 66531
(913) 485-2654
Hostess: Trix Fasse

The inn was constructed at the turn of the century, and has been completely restored. Decorated with antiques, the atmosphere is quaint and homey. There is lots of gingerbread trim on the outside of the house. The parlor is Victorian, with walls and ceiling handpainted with roses. The dining room is papered with quilt blocks. The kitchen is decorated in a 1920's era motif. Two bedrooms have half baths, and one has an old tin ceiling.

Rates: $$ Includes full breakfast. No children or pets, please. Smoking allowed in designated areas.

Magic Peach Cobbler

1 1/2 cups butter
3 cups sugar
3 cups flour
4 1/2 teaspoons baking powder
3 cups milk
1 large can sliced peaches
1 1/2 cups sugar for topping

Melt butter in cake pan. Mix 3 cups sugar, flour, baking powder and milk. Pour over butter in pan. Do not stir. Add peaches on top of this. Place 1 1/2 cups sugar on top of peaches. Bake at 350° for one hour. You may substitute other fruit of your choice. This is very good!

Makes 10 - 12 servings.

Victorian Reflections

820 N.W. Third • Abilene, KS 67410
(913) 263-7774
Hosts: Don and Diana McBride

This prestigious Victorian home is exemplary of the wealth and luxury enjoyed by the successful entrepreneurs of Abilene at the turn of the century. Today, as in the early 1900's, guests can visit and relax in the sun-filled music room and front parlor, or enjoy a book by the fireside in the formal living room. For those who forget a book, many are available in the oak bookcases in the library. In the evening guests will make their way up the beautiful curved stairway to the second floor where four of the home's nine bedrooms are available for use. A full breakfast will be served after which guests may want to take a stroll in Eisenhower Park, which adjoins the Inn property, or just relax on the huge porch and view the many wonderful Victorian homes on Third Street.

Rates: $ - $$$ Includes full breakfast. Children over 10 are welcome. No pets or smoking, please. We accept MasterCard and Visa.

Chocolate Chip Banana Muffins

4 overripe bananas, mashed
1 cup sugar
1/2 cup butter
1 egg
1 teaspoon vanilla extract
2 cups flour
1 teaspoon baking soda
1/2 teaspoon baking powder
1 cup semi-sweet chocolate chips

Beat together bananas, sugar, butter, egg, and vanilla. Mix dry ingredients and add to the banana mixture. Add chocolate chips. Spoon into greased muffin tins and bake at 350° for 25 minutes.

Makes 1 1/2 - 2 dozen.

Wakefield's Country B&B

R.R. #1, Box 212, 197 Sunflower Road • Wakefield, KS 67487
(913) 461-5533
Hosts: Vernon and Kathy Yenni

A touch of country living awaits you at our lovingly restored 1930's home. We are the third generation of our family to live on this diversified grain and livestock farm. We offer quiet country hospitality and a special breakfast. We are a short drive to numerous tourist attractions at Milford Lake, Abilene, Junction City and Manhattan.

Rates: $ Includes full breakfast. Children are welcome. Pets allowed. No smoking, please.

Hamburger Steaks

3 lbs. hamburger
1 cup milk
1 cup cracker crumbs
3 teaspoons salt
Pepper to taste
1 can cream of mushroom soup
Flour for frying

Mix all ingredients except soup and flour. Flatten the meat mixture on jelly roll pan and let stand in refrigerator overnight. Cut meat into serving pieces, dip in flour and brown in hot skillet. Place browned meat in a casserole, cover with soup and bake at 325° for one hour.

Makes 10 - 12 servings.

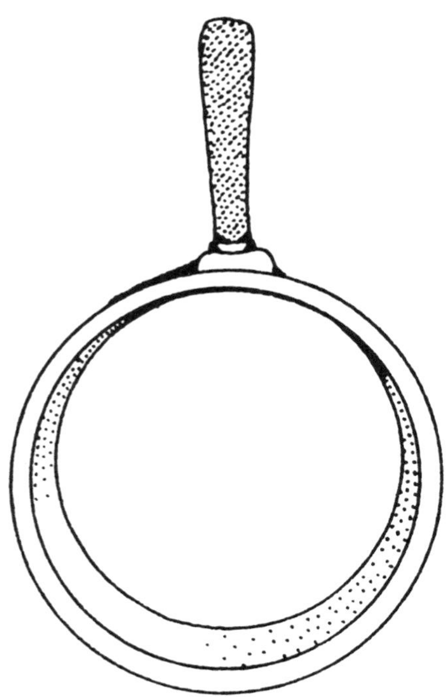

Wallingford Inn

519 Maple, Box 799 • Ashland, KS 67831
(316) 635-2129
Hosts: Aaron and Susan Bates

Enter a bygone era of charm and grace when you visit the Wallingford Inn. The 1910 3-story white frame house was built by early day grain magnate, Charles A. Wallingford. The inn has been elegantly restored with historical furnishings and a light Victorian flair. Each of 4 bedrooms is unique in theme and decor. Guests are served full breakfasts in the elegantly restored dining room. Fresh English scones, cinnamon rolls, or pecan rolls complement a chilled fruit salad, orange juice and fresh coffee. Enjoy sunsets and conversation seated on porch swings on the wraparound veranda. Play an exhilarating game of croquet or relax by strolling through our English garden. All this and more awaits your visit!

Rates: $$ Includes continental plus breakfast. Children over 12 are welcome. No pets or smoking, please.

This scone is considered a British biscuit, served at breakfast or tea time.

British Oatmeal Scones

2/3 cup margarine, melted
1/3 cup milk
1 egg
1 1/2 cups flour
1 1/4 cups quick oats, uncooked
1/2 cup sugar
1 tablespoon baking powder
1/2 teaspoon salt
1/2 teaspoon nutmeg
1 teaspoon cinnamon
1/2 cup raisins

Preheat oven to 425°. Mix dry ingredients. Add butter, milk and egg to dry mixture. Add raisins. Shape dough to form ball and pat out on floured surface to form an 8" circle. Cut into 8 - 12 wedges. Bake on greased cookie sheet for 12 - 15 minutes or until light golden brown. Serve warm with butter, jam or honey.

Makes 8 - 12 scones.

Walnut Brook B&B

R.R. #3, Box 304 • Great Bend, KS 67530
(316) 792-5900 or FAX (316) 792-5848
Hosts: Mike and Janet Hammeke

A storybook country get-a-way. Country English B&B - stately and exclusive with 7 acres of wooded creek nature trails, cottage gardens, patios and spacious green meadow; able to assist with amenities plus - business and social transactions, receptions, club meetings, company picnics, weddings and small dinner parties. Special features: "Murder Mystery at the Inn" weekend Sherlock packages, western entertainment nights, horse-drawn carriage rides, gift shop, large above ground pool, sauna, gym, hot tub mineral spa, fireplace, gourmet cuisine and a new "Just for You" pampering weekend for ladies only at our health spa. 3 rooms plus 2 Santa Fe teepee suites for an overnight camping on the "trail" experience. Breakfast by campfire included (year-round). An enchanting retreat and the feeling you have been royalty for a day!

Rates: $$ Includes full breakfast. Children over 8 are welcome. Pets allowed. No smoking, please.

We bribed the chef from our favorite café in the mountains of Colorado to divulge this recipe! Our guests feel very special and pampered when a soufflé is placed before them. The walnuts fit the theme of Walnut Brook!

Apple & Cheddar Soufflé

1 cup milk
4 tablespoons butter
5 tablespoons flour
1/2 teaspoon cinnamon
Dash of nutmeg
1/2 teaspoon salt
1 tablespoon honey
6 eggs, separated, at room temperature
1 packed cup grated Cheddar cheese
2 cups grated tart apple
1/2 cup finely minced walnuts

Preheat oven to 375°. Generously butter medium soufflé dish. Heat milk slowly in heavy saucepan. Remove from heat just before it boils. Melt butter in medium saucepan. Whisk it, as you gradually sprinkle in flour, keep cooking and whisking the resulting "roux" for another 5 minutes. While whisking, drizzle in still-hot milk. Cook over low heat, stirring steadily with wooden spoon until sauce thickens (8 - 10 minutes). Remove from heat. Stir in spices, salt, and honey. Preheat egg yolks, drizzle them in, beating constantly. Transfer mixture to large bowl. Stir in cheese, apples, and walnuts. Cool to room temperature. Beat egg whites until stiff but not dry. Fold in gently and quickly, with a lifting motion to incorporate air, into the sauce. Turn soufflé into baking dish. Place in preheated oven, reduce heat to 350°, and leave soufflé to bake in total concentration for 40 minutes. Serve 0.0 minutes after removing from oven! Sprinkle powdered sugar and nutmeg at table.

Serves 4 - 6.

The Williams House

526 North 5th Street • Atchison, KS 66002
(913) 367-1757
Hosts: Dixie and Duane Williams

1884 Victorian home featuring three guest rooms furnished with antiques and family heirlooms. To help you feel "at home" during your stay the house also features an elegantly designed formal living room in which to rest, read, or visit. The sun room, with wicker furniture and 3 "walls" of windows, is perfect for viewing television, listening to the stereo, playing the piano or simply enjoying the many green and blooming plants found there. A full breakfast, served in the formal dining room on antique dishes, will accommodate both the healthy and health conscious appetite. Near restaurants and Atchison's historic attractions. Within 30 minutes of Haderway House Restaurant, Pony Express Museum, Weston, MO, (a pre-Civil War town) and Snow Creek ski area.

Rates: $ Includes full breakfast. Children are welcome. No pets or smoking, please. We accept MasterCard and Visa.

I put a plate of these brownies along with a pitcher of iced tea in the guest rooms for a late-night snack.

Brownies

1/3 cup oleo
1 heaping tablespoon cocoa
1 cup sugar
2 eggs
3/4 cup flour, not sifted
1/4 teaspoon baking powder
1/4 teaspoon salt
1 teaspoon vanilla
1/2 cup chopped nuts (opt.)

Grease and flour an 8" x 8" pan. Mix ingredients in order listed. Don't beat very much, just until blended. Pour into pan. Bake at 350° for barely 30 minutes (watch carefully, some ovens take less time). Recipe doubles very well, to be baked in 11" x 15" pan. Glaze with powdered sugar frosting while warm.

8" pan makes 9 brownies.
11" pan makes 18 brownies.

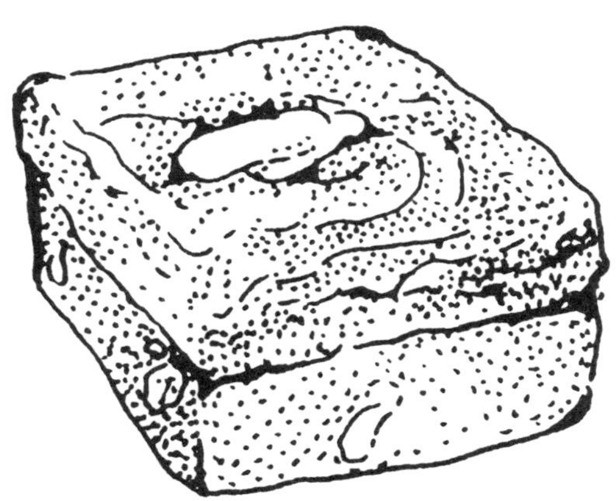

Windmill Inn

Route 1, Box 32 • Chapman, KS 67431 (Abilene)
(913) 263-8755
Hosts: Tim and Deb Sanders

Surrounded by acres of farm ground and nestled near historic Abilene, KS, this bed and breakfast inn recreates the charm of a bygone era. Special attention has been given to every detail of the restoration, down to the beautiful oak woodwork and brilliant stained and beveled glass in the common areas. The wraparound front porch lures you to come enjoy the sights and sounds of country life while relaxing in a porch swing or rocking chair. Four guest rooms, each with its own distinctive amenities and decor, and your stay includes a specially prepared country breakfast. After your day's tour of historical sites or casual drive through some of KS's scenic countryside, return to the Inn for an evening meal that will complete your perfect day.

Rates: $$ Includes full breakfast. Children over 8 are welcome. Pets allowed. No smoking.

This recipe is often served at Windmill Inn for our evening guests, and the plates are ALWAYS clean!

Cheesy Roasted Potatoes

2 lbs. red potatoes
3/4 cup cream
1/2 cup chicken broth
Coarse salt to taste
Cavender's Greek seasoning to taste
1 cup grated Swiss cheese

Scrub and thinly slice red potatoes. Place in 9" x 13" pan sprayed with vegetable spray. Combine cream and chicken broth and pour over potatoes. Sprinkle with coarse salt and Cavender's Greek seasoning. Bake at 350° for one hour, stirring once. Sprinkle Swiss cheese over top and heat until tender and melted.

Makes 6 servings.

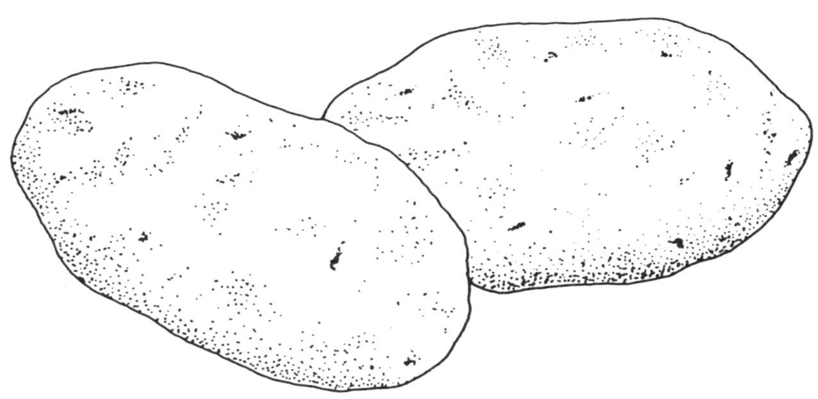

Woody House Bed & Breakfast

Highway 18 & North Street • Lincoln, KS 67455
(913) 524-4744
Hosts: Michael and Ivona Pickering

Our historical 1906 Queen Anne Victorian house offers designer linens, thick towels, comfy beds, strong coffee and a fat, friendly cat! Overnight guests may choose one of three country decorated rooms. A room named Country Comfort overlooks the old Woody produce gardens and apple orchards. The Summer Terrace faces a decorative porch which was used for sleeping in the summer nights before a/c. The Parlour Suite is located in the turret and features an ornate bed, lacy curtains at curved glass windows and a velvet loveseat. Each guest room has a wash basin. A large Victorian bath is shared. Close to country dining, museums, a famous flower-landscaped farm, Lake Wilson, antique and craft shops and the Garden of Eden.

Rates: $ Includes continental breakfast. Please inquire about children in advance. No pets or smoking, please.

Our guests love the aroma of this bread baking at night. The vanilla makes the difference!

Woody House Banana Bread

1 stick butter
1 cup sugar
2 eggs
1 teaspoon baking soda
1 teaspoon salt
1 teaspoon baking powder
2 cups flour (can use half white, half Kansas whole wheat)
1/2 cup buttermilk
1/2 cup chopped walnuts
4 medium mashed bananas
1 - 2 teaspoons vanilla

Mash bananas in separate bowl. Set aside. Cream butter and sugar, beat in eggs. Sift dry ingredients and add, along with the buttermilk. Stir in walnuts, then mashed bananas. Add the vanilla, Michael's secret touch! Bake in 2 lb. greased pan at 350° for 40 minutes. Let cool before slicing.

Makes 16 slices.

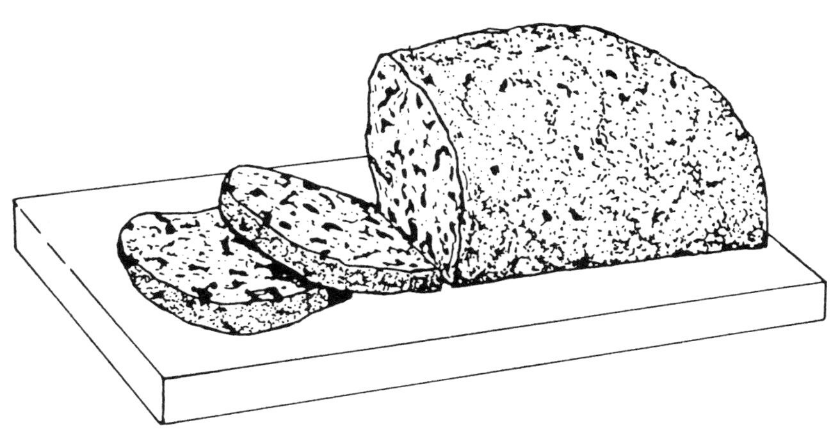

NOTES

NOTES

ORDER FORM

Check for availability at your local bookstore, or indicate the quantity of the book(s) that you wish to order below. Please feel free to copy this form for your order. MAIL THIS ORDER TO:

Winters Publishing
P.O. Box 501
Greensburg, IN 47240

Qty.			
______	*Indiana B&B Assn. Cookbook*	$ 9.95 each	____________
______	*Overnight Sensations*	$ 9.95 each	____________
______	*Pure Gold - Colorado Treasures*	$ 9.95 each	____________
______	*Inn-describably Delicious*	$ 9.95 each	____________
______	*Be Our Guest*	$ 9.95 each	____________
______	*Just Inn Time for Breakfast*	$10.95 each	____________
______	*A Taste of Tennessee*	$ 9.95 each	____________
______	*Sunrise in Kentucky*	$ 9.95 each	____________
______	*Savor the Inns of Kansas*	$ 9.95 each	____________
______	*American Mornings*	$12.95 each	____________
	Shipping Charge	$ 2.00 each	____________
	5% Sales Tax (IN residents ONLY)		____________
		TOTAL	____________

Send to:

Name: ____

Address: ____

City: ____________________ State: ______________ Zip: __________

More Bed & Breakfast Cookbooks from Winters Publishing

The Indiana Bed & Breakfast Association Cookbook and Directory
Features recipes from 75 inns throughout the state of Indiana, with complete information about each inn. 96 pgs. $9.95

Overnight Sensations
Recipes From Virginia's Finest Bed & Breakfasts
Features recipes from 90 inns throughout the state of Virginia, with complete information about each inn. 112 pgs. $9.95

Pure Gold - Colorado Treasures
Recipes From Bed & Breakfast Innkeepers of Colorado
Features more than 100 recipes from 54 inns throughout the state of Colorado, with complete information about each inn. 96 pgs. $9.95

Inn-describably Delicious
Recipes From The Illinois Bed & Breakfast Association Innkeepers
Features recipes from 82 inns throughout the state of Illinois, with complete information about each inn. 112 pgs. $9.95

Be Our Guest
Cooking with Missouri's Innkeepers
Features recipes from 43 inns throughout the state of Missouri, with complete information about each inn. 96 pgs. $9.95

Just Inn Time for Breakfast
A Cookbook from the Michigan Lake To Lake B & B Association
Features recipes from 93 inns throughout the state of Michigan, with complete information about each inn. 128 pgs. $10.95

A Taste of Tennessee
Recipes From Tennessee Bed & Breakfast Inns
Features 80 recipes from 40 inns throughout the state of Tennessee, with complete information about each inn. 96 pgs. $9.95

Sunrise in Kentucky
Breakfast Recipes From Kentucky's Finest Bed & Breakfast Inns
Features over 100 breakfast recipes from 51 inns throughout the state of Kentucky, with complete information about each inn. 112 pgs. $9.95

Savor the Inns of Kansas
Recipes From Kansas Bed & Breakfasts
Features recipes from 51 inns throughout the state of Kansas, with complete information about each inn. 112 pgs. $9.95

American Mornings
Favorite Breakfast Recipes From Bed & Breakfast Inns
Features breakfast recipes from 302 inns throughout the country, with complete information about each inn. 320 pgs. $12.95

INDEX OF BED & BREAKFASTS